C000263610

TEARS
at
NIGHT
JOY AT DAWN

TEARS *at* NIGHT
JOY AT DAWN
Journal of a Dying Seminarian

Andrew Robinson

alive Publishing
www.alivepublishing.co.uk

First published in 2003 by Alive Publishing Ltd.

Second edition published in September 2010

Graphic House, 124 City Road, Stoke on Trent ST4 2PH

Tel: +44 (0) 1782 745600. Fax: +44 (0) 1782 745500

www.alivepublishing.co.uk

©2010 Alive Publishing

British Library Catalogue-in-Publication Date. A catalogue record
for this book is available from the British Library.

All rights reserved. No part of this publication may be reproduced
or transmitted in any form or by any means, electronic or
mechanical, including photocopying, recording or any information
storage and retrieval system, without either prior permission in
writing from the publisher or a licence permitting
restricted copying.

In the United Kingdom such licences are issued by the Publishers
Licensing Society Ltd, 90 Tottenham Court Road,
London W1P 9HE

978-1-906278-10-6

'The presence of God who has been so apparent during the whole of our journey'

'As I sang Hosanna, a tear fell unnoticed from my face. There I was, in all my suffering, happy to sing the praises of God.'

'I feel God is using me in my situation.'

Tears at Night, Joy at Dawn,
Andrew Robinson

The cross reminds us that there is no true love without suffering, there is no gift of life without pain.
Pope Benedict XVI

In a world where there is so much noise, so much bewilderment, there is a need for silent adoration of Jesus concealed in the Host. Be assiduous in the prayer of adoration and teach it to the faithful. It is a source of comfort and light, particularly to those who are suffering.
Pope Benedict XVI

If we let Christ into our lives, we lose nothing, nothing, absolutely nothing of what makes life free, beautiful, and great. No! Only in this friendship are the doors of life opened wide. Only in this friendship is the great potential of human existence truly revealed.
Pope Benedict XVI

*Faith teaches us that we should no longer live under the
fear of death because of what Christ has done.
Our hope and prayer is that Andrew's journal may help many
who are suffering or dying from cancer. The love and support
we have known is carrying us through the pain of our loss.
God bless you all.*

The Robinson family

Many thanks to Archbishop Vincent Nichols
who sent me this little notebook to encourage
me to continue to write my diary entries
and reflections.

Andrew Robinson

CD Contents

- Archbishop Vincent Nichols, Archbishop of Westminster explains the inspiration which made him invite Andrew to write his journal.

- Listen to Andrew Robinson practising a talk he gave before he died on how his faith and the support of so many gave him strength and courage to face his ordeal.

- Enjoy the singing of Andrew's favourite psalm, Psalm 29 led by Monsignor Mark Crisp, Rector of St Mary's College, Oscott, Birmingham and the 9.00 O'clock Sunday Mass Choir from St Thomas More Parish, Coventry.

Contents

Introduction

ANDREW ROBINSON KNEW that God was calling him to be a priest. He responded generously to this call and entered St Mary's College, Oscott, Birmingham in October 1997. He was 26, a qualified surveyor with a good job, a girlfriend, a house and a successful career ahead of him. His decision to begin his training was rooted in prayer, reflection and struggle. Talented and vivacious he knew how to live life to the full. Andrew was popular, academic and loved sport – gifted in so many ways with a love for people and a zest for life.

In July 2000 his life changed forever – Andrew was diagnosed with cancer of the colon. The news was earth-shattering to him, his family and friends; the anguish and shock palpable. The prognosis was not good – the cancer (rare in young men) was advanced and growing. A course of painful chemotherapy and treatment followed and he began his fight for life.

Archbishop Vincent Nichols invited him to keep a journal and record his journey as he embraced God's will. *Tears at Night, Joy at Dawn – Journal of a Dying Seminarian* is an eloquent, profound and deeply moving testimony on one man's journey towards death. Andrew's faith that God had a plan for his life combined with his conviction that he lived in God's presence is a powerful testimony to his faith in the resurrection. Andrew's insight will comfort, console and encourage: 'As you get closer and closer to the finish line you feel the exhilaration, you begin to smile and shed a tear of joy, one final push and you cross the line. You enter that light in all its glory. Death is that moment of transition when, please God, I will be fully reunited to the Father.'

Andrew died at home on 27 April 2001. His funeral was attended by over 1000 people. *Tears at Night, Joy at Dawn* is a beautiful book about faith in the face of adversity, hope in the face of suffering and love for God in the face of death. Andrew's journal inspires the heart, encourages faith and gives hope – we rejoice in this witness and thank God for his life.

Preface

IN LATE DECEMBER 2000 I went to visit Andrew Robinson at his home in Coventry. This was my first opportunity to meet and talk with him since the diagnosis of cancer. I had heard a great deal about his courage and cheerfulness in the face of his life-threatening illness, and about the remarkable way in which he spoke publicly about the experience of sickness and pain which he was sharing with so many other people.

It was during that evening that I asked Andrew if he would keep a journal of the days ahead and of his journey of faith. I said I was sure that both he, and others, would draw strength from it.

Little did I know how rich a gift he would leave us.

Now, of course, I am very grateful to Andrew for writing this journal. I am grateful to his family and friends for agreeing to its publication. I am especially grateful to Mike and Sue Conway of Alive Publishing for having the vision and drive to ensure that Andrew's journal was first published and then widely distributed.

Reading this journal opens for us a remarkable account of joyful faith in the heart and actions of a young man. Here is a moving testimony of the life-giving grace of God at work in our midst. Andrew has written in a candid and humorous manner, which makes his faith and joy accessible to us all.

Since the launch of *Tears at Night, Joy at Dawn* in March 2003 I have received hundreds upon hundreds of letters from people all around the world who wrote to me to tell me how reading Andrew's journal struck a deep chord in so many ways. Some were struggling with cancer themselves, others were considering a vocation to the priesthood or the religious life and many simply found Andrew's humble and courageous witness a wonderful encouragement in living out their faith in the world today, (see Letters, page 109).

This second edition has the added feature of a CD with Andrew practising a talk he gave about how his faith in God and the support of so many around him gave him the grace and strength to face his trial and suffering.

Also on the CD Monsignor Mark Crisp, Rector of St Mary's College Oscott, Birmingham and the St Thomas More Parish, Coventry, Sunday Mass 9.00am Choir sing Psalm 29, the Psalm that inspired the title of *Tears at Night, Joy at Dawn*, which Monsignor Mark composed and sang at Andrew's funeral Mass.

As you come to the end of this journal you will learn that Andrew died a holy death. I am sure that he will be supporting us all with his prayers. Above all he will be urging God to bless all those who give themselves unstintingly to God's service, especially as Catholic priests. And he will be asking God to give an extra prompt to those young men who, like himself, are gradually coming to know that their true and lasting joy will be found in the priesthood.

Finally, I would like to extend an invitation again to those who on reading this second edition or on listening to the CD are moved, touched or encouraged in some way to write to me at Archbishop's House, Ambrosden Avenue, London, SW1. I will be glad to hear from you.

✠ Vincent

✠ Vincent Nichols
Archbishop of Westminster
September 2010

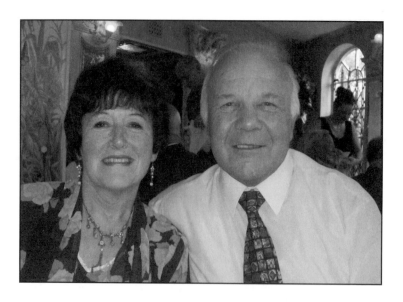

Clive and Stella Robinson

A Reflection

IT IS NINE YEARS now since Andrew died. There isn't a day that passes without us wishing he was with us. We can still feel his joy and enthusiasm in reaching out to others. He had so much energy, enthusiasm and zest for life. He loved serving others, especially those in need of a helping hand or needing to be reassured that God was with them. The sick, the lonely, the elderly, and those in need always remember him. Andrew always had time for people.

We still miss him so much and the pain of his absence has not gone away. We have to remind each other that he has gone back to the Lord, and, through his journal and now this second edition is still able to encourage and support others in living their faith. The Lord gave him to us, he was a gift, and we were so blessed to have thirty two very happy years with him.

None of us expect to bury our children and losing Andrew was the hardest thing we have faced as a family. However, through the gift of faith, the support of our family, our many dear friends and the parish of St Thomas More, Coventry, we have somehow found the strength and the grace to endure a grief which, in truth, cannot be spoken.

We have always found great comfort and consolation from the following words of St Thomas More, in a letter he wrote to his daughter Margaret, on July 5 1535, the day before his execution:

'Farewell, my dear child, and pray for me, and I shall for you and all your friends, that we may merrily meet in heaven.'

This is our prayer too, that one day we will be united with our dear son who we love so much and miss so dearly.

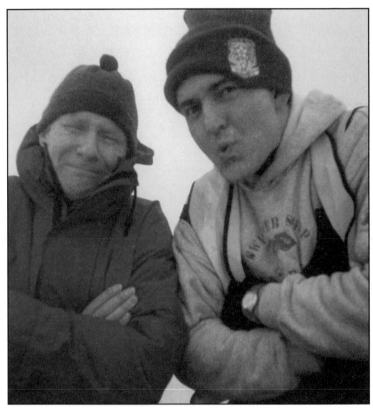

Andrew out hiking on Skiddaw with John Bentley

Climbing Skiddaw

17 JANUARY 2001

IN FEBRUARY 1999, 'The Famous Five' undertook a ridiculous challenge to climb 931 metres up Skiddaw, near Keswick, in the Cumbrian mountains (Lake District), at night! The idea was to arrive at the summit in time for sunrise, at which time we would sing God's praise and say Morning Prayer. As with most adventures things didn't go quite according to plan. The wind was exceptionally fierce and John, Katy, Roger, Thanh and myself made the mistake of challenging it. The story is recounted in the *Oscotian* 1999 edition, the title being 'Not Quite the Spiritual Journey We Had Expected'. At the top we had all linked arms in an attempt to plod together to the summit. Katy was flapping about like a kite between me and John as she was so light; we clung on to her tightly as a gust would have sent her up and away like leaves on a windy day. On the plateau we were totally unprotected from the raw power and severity of the wind at its strongest. We leant against it horizontal, in fact sliding on the stony surface of the mountain top. We had reached our limit; the roofless igloo-type shelters which existed somewhere on the plateau were too far away by a matter of a few yards, although in the dark and mist we could not see them. We lay on the floor of the plateau on top of the mountain, the wind eager to prise us up off the floor and away into the black abyss. I clung on to Katy. 'You're not going anywhere,' I shouted as the wind's efforts to blow her away frightened her. Katy's outer hood shot off her head like a bullet from a gun and I tried to protect her remaining woolly hat from completely exposing her to the biting wind. I began to pray the Hail Mary, not wanting to move in case I broke the inertia which was stopping us being swept away. Within a couple of minutes the darkness gave way to a glimmer of light. The sun had risen. John, Roger and Thanh had crawled a little way off the summit, and as the wind had given its worst, I tentatively wriggled off the summit of the mountain, clinging on to Katy. We regrouped and steadily made our way to the safety of the fence surrounding the base of the mountain top. As we sat in the shelter, behind a sub peak, I got out my Morning and Evening Prayer Book and we read: 'I will praise you, Lord, you have rescued me...' Psalm 29. We laughed at how appropriate the psalm was and out of a certain degree of relief!!

Little did I know, at that time, of how significant a part of my prayer that that psalm would become. I have said it, generally with my family, every day since I was diagnosed with cancer on 19 July 2000. For me, it seems to sum it all up – my need of God, my hopes, my feelings, both the desolation and despair, as well as the consolation and hope and joy. Of course, I ask for healing with hope and faith, but I also ask for the strength to accept God's will for me and to carry my cross with a spirit of joy and thanksgiving that God will draw me and the souls of those around me ever closer to himself and each other.

My irregular diary entries have recorded some of my thoughts and feelings. I guess largely for my own benefit, as I journey through life. They have always been authentic and real and, above all, I hope they continue to be so. Because, perhaps, this may be read by others, as Archbishop Vincent has encouraged me to write, there is a temptation to edit my mind's thoughts. I hope I do not succumb to such doctoring.

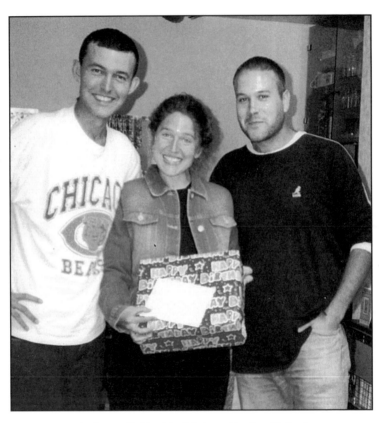

Andrew with his sister Maria and brother Richard

No End in Sight

20 JANUARY 2001

IT'S LATE, BUT while it's quiet and I'm not in too much pain, I thought I would add a few notes. I have had a fantastic Christmas. I had a week off for good behaviour and I was able to get to see a lot of friends. My diary records the events of people I saw and places I went. It was a very blessed time, especially the full Christmas dinner I was able to eat, including cranberry sauce and a special apple crumble which Mum made for me, with soya marg. It was delicious!

However, since then, things have been pretty tough for me. On January 2, I remember travelling to the Q.E., driving in the car. I really did not want to go – how much longer was I going to be able to cope with this chemo treatment? The thought of how I would feel, etc. The fact of it being a new year – the start of a new year, the start of more treatment without an end in sight. However, God does not leave us stranded. His love for me that day came through Anna, who met me at the hospital and stayed with me all day.

We had a few laughs playing cards and she helped me take my mind off things. That week was bad. January 2 was Richard's birthday, and we all went to *The Plough* – Mum, Dad, Nana, Sarah, Richard and me. I was connected up to chemo and quite tired after a long day. But the meal was lovely and the treatment hadn't settled in. By Wednesday, I was in a lot of pain until Sunday/Monday. I remember going to Mass. I sat at the front right of the church, too drained to sit next to people I knew, too drained to put on a smiley face all through Mass. As I sang Hosanna, a tear fell unnoticed from my face. There I was, in all my suffering, happy to sing the praises of God. And I was happy, for in suffering was a sacrifice truly pleasing to God. I felt I was in communion with Christ on the cross in a special way and completely in need of his mercy and healing.

The following week I recovered well. John came to visit me on Tuesday, and we went out for lunch and saw *Charlie's Angels* at the Odeon, which I found really cheesy. That evening I went to Fr Mark's place at Oscott, thanks to the courtesy of Caroline's taxi service for the Matfriscan prayer meeting. Wednesday night was the highlight of my week

– Katy had got me tickets to see *The Corrs* at the National Exhibition Centre in Birmingham. Before the concert we went for a romantic dinner at *The Harvester*. We discussed babies' names to which I advanced my preferences of Zachariah for a boy and Anna for a girl. Katy preferred Zachary and Jessica – yet again we fought our stubborn corners laughing at various ridiculous options. Afterwards, we headed off to the concert. *The Corrs* were extremely talented musicians, but not really entertainers. It was a great concert and afterwards we made our way to the car park and home. A lovely evening – it was nice we could enjoy each other's company as friends without falling prey to the pain of the sacrifice of future marriage. The disappointment or even resentment would often manifest itself in fights, but not tonight. That night was beautiful.

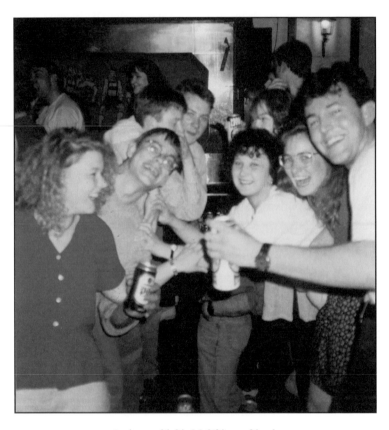

Andrew with his Maltfriscan friends

A Hidden Despair

28 JANUARY 2001

I HAVE OFTEN contemplated my own funeral. For some months I have considered the possibility of producing a few words on video which could perhaps be played. I have often thought that I should say some words of thanks to my united family of God who have all been praying so fervently for my healing. I have wanted to explain how much I have enjoyed my life, how I look forward to heaven and how I wish my family to live in faith that they may join the heavenly host and experience the mercy of God, which I hope to know in all its fullness. I wish to reassure them all that their prayers, especially to Cardinal John Henry Newman (see p.109), have not been in vain, but rather, in union with my suffering and through the cross of Christ, they have, as acts of love, contributed towards the salvation of souls.

I am so looking forward to going to San Giovanni Rotondo next week.[†] God, I feel, has spared me, that I may

† see Appendix 1

visit the home of the great saint whose life's work was the salvation of souls through his suffering. He is, Padre Pio, a true hero of mine. One graced by God to be an instrument of his love to so many of God's people, that they may experience in every way the mercy of God. That we may be free to love, free physically, emotionally, mentally and spiritually.

Over the last few weeks since Christmas especially, I have felt my cancer spread a little up the centre of my front towards my chest. Perhaps God wants me to undergo the full effect of this disease and share in Christ's suffering to the end. Part of me has found it difficult to accept this possibility and it has resulted in a hidden type of despair, because it means that this life holds no hope of experiencing the joy of a physical healing. A kind of resignation sets in – a kind of grieving. Although, please God, I will be happy and joyful and at peace, in full unity with God in the next life, there is so much I appreciate and love in this life – both people and creation. This, no matter how wonderful the next life will be; I can't help but grieve the leaving behind of those I love. I think this is the cause of despair when thinking that God may wish to take me. As the pain seems to persist, this hidden low feeling exists. Hidden, because I only want others to feel strength which also exists within me, because I want those around me to be strong in faith, that God does not desert us. I know God is with me; my low feelings do not remove or mitigate this knowledge and source of strength. I fear that should others know my low feelings, they may feel that I am losing faith, and so lose faith themselves.

However, on Thursday Kath Ryan came round. She does aromatherapy and massage to help me relax after undergoing each treatment session. She comes round during the later half of my 'good week'. (Treatment lasts 48 to 60 hours, once every two weeks. The second of the two weeks – my recovery or good week.) I asked her if she would just put oil on my tummy and pray over it because massaging my tummy tensed me up, because it is tender, and I felt is was spreading the cancer around, even though it most likely wasn't. As Kath prayed over my tummy, I prayed intensely too, for healing and protection from evil and asking the angels and saints to watch over me and intercede for me. I didn't feel anything, particularly, but I sensed that the praying had helped. I sensed a hope and an assertion that it was still important and OK to ask for healing. A reassurance that, no matter what, God wants to heal me. I may not know that healing in this life, at least physically, but that doesn't matter.

In recent days, I felt awkward – should I ask for healing if God doesn't want to heal me? If it is his will that I suffer, am I being selfish, I thought, and if he does want me to suffer, until the end, what's the point in asking for healing? I had a renewed sense that yes, it was OK, and good to continue to ask for healing. Why? Because with healing comes peace and joy, whether I am physically healed or not, and if I have low feelings I need healing!! So I will continue to hope and trust in the Lord for with true healing of body, soul and spirit comes true happiness and until that true happiness of peace and joy comes, I am in need of healing.

*'O Lord, I cried to you for help and you, my God,
have healed me'.*

*I trust and hope in you, my God. I pray, Lord that
you will come to my aid, that you will heal me, that I
may know true happiness and joy with you and be in
perfect harmony with your love. Heal me, Lord, heal me!
That I may, in union with the angels and saints, recognise
and praise your name for ever. Pour out your love, too,
on your children, Lord, that we may sing together
of your love for us, now and forever.
Amen.*

The Church of St Maria in Palazzola

From Hell to Paradise

4 FEBRUARY 2001

WHAT A ROLLERCOASTER of a few days I have had. I am sitting in bed in room 9 at Palazzola, the villa overlooking the lake and the Pope's holiday home on the mountain above Rome. It's a bit dark now and not so warm unless you're in bed like me, all snuggled up. In summer, particularly, it is very hot, perhaps spring and autumn are the best months, but here is a taste of heaven – peaceful, restful, away from the hustle and bustle of the so-called 'real world', a sort of tranquillity is evident, and so, so appreciated!

When I think that yesterday I was in the pit of despair, wherein the cross of Christ is most vividly made real in all its horror and pain and rawness. I was in Ward 1 of the Oncology Unit at the Q.E. Unfortunately, my PICC line which runs in my vein, from my left elbow to my chest, packed up. My chemo pump is connected to it, but the poisonous substance wasn't going in properly, some

33

blockage or narrowing of the vein, had inhibited the flow. I informed the Q.E. and they had me in Thursday 6.00pm. I arrived and told the nurse at the desk my name and that I was booked in for the honeymoon suite. She laughed and led me to my bed which was reference B2 – I was sandwiched between two beds with three parallel beds opposite. To my left was a Japanese man, very elderly who was very weak and waiting to die. Half of Japan congregated round his bed with various daughters keeping vigil overnight.

Another lived on the opposite left, from Southport about 70 to 75 – his wife stayed with him and had a bed in staff quarters. Opposite me was poor old Roger, hardly any visitors and he suffered dreadfully with a pipe coming out of the throat, unable to speak. He constantly coughed up gunge through it and was fed drugs through a line at his pelvis. He, too, must have been in his late seventies, eighties, as was Harry next to him. I'm not sure of his name, actually, but he had two very nice daughters, who I met in the day room. Next to me on my right was Gary who arrived on Friday. He seemed relatively OK, a man in his forties, has a son who played for the Birmingham Youth team, but he was a Villa fan – boooo! (Andrew was an avid Coventry City fan).

So there I was, struggling myself with an IV (intravenous) line machine attached, feeling sickish and weak and generally unwell, placed in communion with four men over twice my age, suffering greatly. There was coughing, wheezing, choking, vomiting, belching, (snoring occasionally when they were able to sleep). The personal TVs went on at 500 decibels because they couldn't hear. At night lamps floodlit the whole ward with light strong enough to cater for a football stadium. Oxygen pumps chugged away all through the night, as did the nebulizers. At all hours of the night nurses shouted at a deaf patient, 'You all right?' 'Do you want the toilet?' 'OK darling, we're here!'

And after a night of no sleep and sheer exhaustion, the morning shift of nurses and caterers arrived, charging in with 'Hi-di-hi campers!' 'Do you want tea love?' 'Have you got a smile for me, sweetheart?!' 'Is that one sugar or two?!' etc. Then it's pills, then breakfast comprising of a few cornflakes and dry stale bread with a tub of flavoured sugar called jam. Then the visitors of the Japanese man would arrive, who were lovely, but loud and numerous. And so it went on. When attached to a line, your only means of escape are the day room and the toilet. When the doctor came round, I asked if there was any chance of speeding the flow rate of chemo so that I could leave Friday evening. 'Sorry, we can do it for Saturday morning.' 'Oh, no,' I thought, 'another night at Alcatraz!'

Dad phoned Friday night and said he would come to pick me up between 10 and 11 am. 'You couldn't make it 8 and 9am?' I pleaded. When he arrived the following day I was packed, ready to go. As we left I said to Dad, 'I've been here two nights and it feels like two years.' With the intravenous line, I couldn't leave the ward and so leaving that morning it felt like the war was over and I was being led out of the concentration camp to freedom. But, oh, how I felt for those left behind. The look on Hilda's face as I left, both of envy of me, and despair of the fact that she would still be in there for a while, said it all! As she sat on the end of her bed with her wig on the sideboard, I wanted to stay and console her, but I couldn't.

We spoke and she wished me a lovely trip to San Giovanni. I said that I'd be thinking and praying for her. She raised a gentle smile and I was gone. How did Cardinal Bernardin of Chicago do it? A sufferer of cancer, who was able to be in hospital and visit all the patients of the ward, ministering to them. All I could do was be tolerant, and chat occasionally to people in the day room with both patients and visitors hanging on to my excitement of going to San Giovanni, which I shared with most people that I spoke to, and the fact that soon my PICC line and intravenous line would be out and I would be out of the pit of despair, in which the cross of Christ was so harshly manifest in those around me and which I felt so much a part of.

Yesterday, Kath helped me to relax with an aromatherapy massage. Dad cooked for me and packed for me. He was my knight in shining armour. After a long day, we said prayers and after Match of the Day we said goodnight.

Today I have experienced so much love. Fr Mark came round at 8.30am. We had Mass with Dad, and Kath came round after with gluten- and dairy-free muffins and carrot cake. That girl has a heart of gold. After spending three to four hours with me chatting, helping me to relax, letting me sleep for an hour or two while she chatted to my dad, she thought she left too early and should have given me more time! And all I could give to Hilda in hospital on my way out was a couple of minutes!! I feel so inadequate when subject to such love. We drove to Fr Mervyn's and so Jane, Maggie and Lou, Pete and Collette popped in to see me before Mass. So many had sent their love through Mervyn.

Within seven hours we were at Palazzola with everything taken care of and going smoothly to plan. The sisters here even left spare pillows outside my room in case I needed them. Fr Pat Kilgarriff met us and looked after us over dinner, and now here I am in bed after being truly pampered. Neither Mervyn nor Mark would let me carry anything, for fear of the many who were concerned for my welfare, giving them strict instructions to look after me. From hell to paradise! The contrast and extremes of these two opposing experiences is beyond words, and yet God has been present so vividly through and in them both.

O Lord, my God, I thank you and praise you for the intensity of despair and love which I have experienced over the last few days. I thank you for the hope and the strength to cope with my small sufferings, and with being in the presence of great suffering. O God, have mercy on me a sinful and weak man. My inadequacy, in the face of the cross, is truly apparent, and above all I ask for your grace and mercy in this respect.

O Lord, watch over all those in Ward 1 of the Q.E. tonight, spare them, Lord, grant them healing, strength and peace. In your name I pray that they will come to know the healing power of your love, especially Hilda, Arthur, Roger, Harry, Gary, Sue, Akka and the Japanese man. Thank you for the generosity of the nurses and doctors, who witness so incredibly to the Good News of your love for all your people.

Bless Frs Mervyn and Mark, Kath and all of the parish of St Thomas More and St Hugh of Lincoln and the Mayor of Woodstock, Ian Lenagan, who have made possible this taste of paradise.

Padre Pio – I am coming with the love and blessing of so many people. Through your intercession, please let God's healing love come to me through you, and in turn be granted to all those who have loved me so dearly, that you may be revered and blessed by God and that God, Father, Son and Holy Spirit, be praised now and for ever more.

Holy, holy, holy, Lord, God of power and might! Heaven and earth are full of your GLORY!! Hosanna in the highest!!!

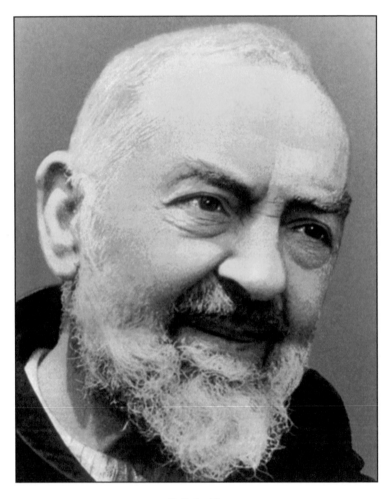

St Padre Pio

St Padre Pio

5 FEBRUARY 2001

WELL HERE I am at last, at the home of Padre Pio in San Giovanni Rotondo. Again, we've had the perfect day. I have had a few pains, but not as sick as normal. After being woken by a few riotous Italian cleaners who talk above one another and never come up for air, I got up and went down with Mark and Mervyn for 9.30 am Mass. An overcast day, but beautiful all the same. We said Morning Prayer in Mervyn's room and then down for breakfast in the little sitting room, overlooking Lake Albano. Fr Pat timed his entrance to perfection, and we went out to the garden for photos, one of which was done on the self-timer, with the camera precariously perched on the side of a chair on a table. We said goodbye to the sisters, one of whom was Sr Gertrude, only the second Gertrude I have ever met in my life, the first living in a convent in Rearsby, a village outside Leicester, where I lived between the ages of two and four. My earliest memories are of going to visit Sr Gertrude and praying for her as she was very old.

At 11.40 am we set off for the destination of our pilgrimage. We passed Montecassino and St Benedict's monastery, Aquino where St Thomas Aquinas was born, Mount Vesuvius eventually, as the first Mount Vesuvius which Mark pointed out turned out to be a quarry! After taking a slight detour, we arrived at the foothills of the mountains holding San Giovanni. They appeared huge in contrast to the flat land of olive trees and grape vines which marked our approach. The setting sun cast orange glows on the rocks as we drove to what turned out to be a vibrant, rather large town, and not the quaint, somewhat backward little village I had anticipated. A security man drove ahead of us and led us to our lodgings. A police car also happened to be clearing the way ahead. It was like a planned Padre Pio welcome. The rooms were cold, but lovely, and we met Antonio Lucia and his wife, Enrica, who were friends of Antonio, who I had met in Coventry and ten years later in Kidlington. His aunt ensured our rooms were spotless and Antonio took us to a lovely restaurant which catered for both mine and Mervyn's dietary requirements. Mark told us that he used to eat dog food, but didn't like Winalot, and Mervyn apparently ate wallpaper paste when he was a kid! And they both had the nerve to be fascinated by the strange eccentricities of a George McFly character (from the *Back to the Future* film) who sat behind us! After a lovely meal, which I could only eat a little of, we went back to our accommodation for Night Prayer. Thank you, Padre Pio, and all who are praying for me, for the journey and the welcome I have received, and the smoothness of the journey which has been inspiring in itself. To think I know Antonio who happens to be from San Giovanni, Frs Mervyn and Mark, who both speak Italian, which has been absolutely invaluable when we were stopped by the police, and at the restaurant. Every need has been met without fail. Even Fr Pat Kilgarriff who arranged our free (they wouldn't take anything) accommodation at Palazzola. Also, to Gerry Bradley who introduced me to the great man, and to all at Kidlington and the Mayor Woodstock, all of whom helped pay for me to go. If I wasn't ill, none of this truly wonderful experience would have happened. Thank you!!

Tomorrow, I look forward to going to the convent and Padre Pio's monastery and chapel. As we said the Joyful Mysteries, we prayed for all the above, as well as all the sick back home. We prayed especially for Richard, Karl and Mandy; Ann Fellows who is seriously ill now; and Steve Rooney who died last Tuesday night, an event which truly upset me – so quick and so final. But in hope and trust, I have arrived in communion with all those above and pray for God's grace and mercy. Alleluia!

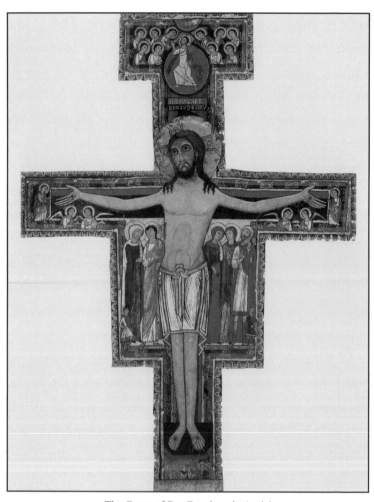

The Cross of San Damiano in Assisi

The Cross
6 FEBRUARY 2001

WHAT A FANTASTIC and blessed day we have had. I was struggling with the cold last night, and with stomach cramps. Mark and Mervyn came in at about 10.00 am after having been shopping for cereal, soya milk, disposable plates and cutlery, bread and prunes! We all had a lovely breakfast in my room and, then, fast shower to warm up, Morning Prayer and up to the church. We met a Friar whom Antonio had told us to see and he immediately arranged for us to say Mass in the private chapel where Padre Pio said Mass, when prevented from doing so by the authorities, while they investigated his stigmata. What an honour! In God's providence all events had brought us to be at this place of blessing with such ease. I read the first reading (Gen 1:1-25) – the creation story – and Mark read the Gospel. Afterwards, we said a decade of the rosary and I remember distinctly the beautiful, but sad, statue of Our Lady looking down at me with loving eyes.

We prayed at the tomb; saw the crucifix before which Padre Pio received the stigmata; saw the chapel where he said Mass and the people flocked in to witness and take part; the new church adjacent to where a beautiful mosaic of Our Lady with the Child Jesus at her breast adorns the back of the altar.

Good old St Anthony of Padua's altar and statue resides at the side. The huge basilica is seen at the rear of the church, still under construction, and the Way of the Cross and hospital, also huge, is at the front, facing down the mountainside. We had a beautiful picnic lunch of peanut butter sandwiches and carrot cake on the mountainside in the sunshine overlooking the rolling green hills, with cowbells breaking the peace down below. Beautiful! After a siesta we toured the church and corridors, bought books, listened to Padre Pio (awaiting the statue of Our Lady of Fatima and calling people to pray) on the phone and said the rosary and Vespers with the friars in church. We had a lovely pasta and fish meal whilst chatting over and laughing about embarrassing moments, including the one of me greeting a Conservative canvasser at the door with toilet roll hanging out the back of my trousers! Compline and a discussion on the cross and suffering was also a highlight at the end of the day.

Unless we come to understand the Cross, all that Christ was about cannot be comprehended and nor can much of our own life. Padre Pio helps greatly in witnessing to the value of suffering and the contribution it makes to salvation of souls through the Cross of Christ. What an honour to be able to live a life by which many would come to experience the mercy of God. When suffering and asking for healing, our motivation can be so much like the bad thief – something which I have recognised in me for some time – 'Save yourself, Lord, and me too if you are the Son of God' (Luke 23:29). In other words, healing – physical healing – is purely for the glory of God and so that I might witness to the truth, not so that by-the-way I can be spared from a nasty death, and carry on living the life of Riley. My motivation is so often to be released from pain and suffering so that I can live on and enjoy life, rather than desiring the will of God, whether that be to offer up my suffering like Padre Pio until the cancer kills me, or experience the healing hand of God, so that God is glorified and I can conscientiously carry on fulfilling his will in the future. Either way, in both cases, God is to be glorified, and, please God, through suffering, in communion with the Cross of Christ, souls are saved.

Yes, as I have indicated before, it is still right and fitting to ask for healing, both physical and spiritual, but most importantly the latter – that my motivation be that of the good thief, and not the bad thief, that I may be at peace and happiness in both the joys and sufferings of life, but especially in the sufferings, in which one wills to love in a truly privileged way as Padre Pio did, as a follower of Christ and one who participated so fully in the greatest saving act of love – that of the Cross. The former physical healing is either a joyful taste of the resurrection in this life for the glory of God or it is reserved for the next in all its fullness.

'Heal me, Lord, that I may be at one with you, that either way I may accept suffering for love of you and neighbour, with peace and joy. As I continue on my journey to you, I feel at times that this prayer is being answered more and more, not in a smooth progression, but with lots of ups and downs. Keep me with you, Lord, that I may 'walk the walk', for without you I am lost. I ask this in the name of your Son who lights up the path and leads me on as the example to follow and the friend to be with. Thank you for your presence with me in the love of both Mark and Mervyn and the example and love and prayers of my friends, Padre Pio and St Anthony of Padua.'

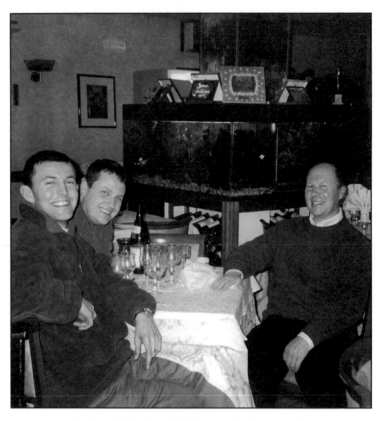

Andrew, Fr Mark and Fr Mervyn enjoying a meal at
San Giovanni

St Michael's Grotto

7 FEBRUARY 2001

WE HAD ANOTHER beautiful and blessed day. This morning we journeyed to Mount San Angelo, the oldest shrine to St Michael the Archangel. What a beautifully peaceful place. The town was old with white buildings, narrow steep streets and roll-tiled roofs all on top of one another. The church was cold and we went down to the grotto where the apparition of St Michael had taken place. As soon as we entered through the gate at the bottom of the stairs into the chamber, the atmosphere hit us. At the back of the cave was an altar with a Franciscan cross to the left and a statue of St Michael encased in a glass cabinet with gold columns at the corners and a red surround. The lighting was such that you couldn't help gazing upon it. I went up to the back of the cave to the left of the altar and prayed the rosary for Katy and her family; for the sick whom I named; for my immediate family; for me and for those who had died – Nana, Grandad, etc. I was just in time to get some finger rosaries blessed on the altar and the church closed for siesta.

We had a steady walk around the beautiful town overlooking a steep drop to the Adriatic Sea. Then we headed off and found a place for a picnic under a tree up another mountain where Mervyn sang 'A Partridge in a Pear Tree' in order to mark a historic event in the life of this extremely tranquil part of the world. Mark picked a few crocuses that weren't for pressing and after photos of San Angelo opposite in the distance and jam sandwiches (because I had forgotten the peanut butter), we headed off for a siesta.

Then it was off to the church and the tomb of Padre Pio for Mass for the intention of St Thomas More and St Hugh of Lincoln, Kidlington and the Maltfriscan Community. I read to an audience of Italians in English! Then I sang the Alleluia and a few of them were able and kind enough to join in. Poor Mark was nervous in addressing the Italians, so didn't, but as is wonderful about the Mass, the Liturgy did the work. It was a prayerful time, but perhaps not the occasion for a healing.

We returned to the tomb after Mass for prayers and on entering the big church, we were straight back down on our knees again for Benediction. Afterwards, a poor old man tripped over the back of my legs, Mervyn fell in love with the woman in the choir with a green tea-cosy on her head and off we went for yet more gifts for those back home. Fr Rinaldo, who had looked after us so well with regard to the Masses, gave us biscuits as we left and said goodnight to one of many good-looking volunteers – girls who kept vigil at the door. We said Evening Prayer, by which time it was an in-joke that Mark kept yawning during every prayer time, saying the Office and that perhaps he needed exorcising. I phoned Dad, full of news, and then chatted to Antonio Marcucci in Milan. Antonio Lucia, his best friend, took us to see Mr and Mrs Marcucci for tea and then we found a real local restaurant complete with stone walls and football Italiana in a room no bigger than a large living room. After a lovely meal during which Mervyn had both pig, cheese (and horse!) we went home, phoned Maggie Borucki to check the parish was OK and said Night Prayer during which Mark yawned again – mind you after a full day – so did I!!

Mittens worn by Padre Pio over his stigmatic hands

My Blessed Day

10 FEBRUARY 2001

WOW! WHAT AN incredible last day I had on Thursday. After breakfast we went up to do the Way of the Cross next to the church. The Stations were not as impressive as Lourdes, but very beautiful bronze scenes set in stone frames, all surrounded by trees. At the fifth station Mark thought he was having a religious experience until Mervyn pointed out a scented incense stick smouldering from the plant bed. The fourth station, always my favourite, of Jesus meeting his mother, was especially powerful and the fifth station of Simon of Cyrene carrying Jesus' cross was interesting/ poignant because Simon was in the form of Padre Pio in Franciscan habit. The last three stations – Jesus dies, is taken down and the resurrection – were very emotional as the words of Padre Pio from his 'Stations of Cross' took on a special significance for me and for Mark and Mervyn. After we finished praying, we took some strategic photos and then headed off for lunch, being careful to avoid the trappings of a certain gypsy lady who was confusing the message of Padre Pio by handing out prayer cards and lucky charms and then trying to sting me for extortionate sums of money. Fortunately, Mervyn got me out of trouble earlier on that morning and we side-stepped her on our way back to the car. She kind of sat by the car park entrance like a Venus flytrap, coaxing her prey!

We drove inland past a monastery, into some woods and found a lovely picnic area for yet more peanut butter sandwiches with cheese and jam, followed by Kath's sacred carrot cake, which was still sustaining us. Actually, I forgot the peanut butter that day, but it didn't deter us from having another perfect lunch in the sun.

No I didn't, it was the day before I forgot the peanut butter. No wonder I had to stop. My brain was failing more than normal! After our regular siesta we headed off back to the convent (not just for sisters/nuns, but also for friars. In Italy, monasteries are for Friars of an enclosed order).

That afternoon was to be the climax par excellence to an already truly blessed pilgrimage. We went in to the sacristy as normal, and got ready for Mass which would be said in the church where Padre Pio said daily Mass, ie: the old church. We went through into the original sacristy where Padre Pio would have prepared for Mass and through on to the other sanctuary of the church. Of course, the altar was fixed to the back wall. Fr Mervyn and Fr Mark had to say Mass facing the tabernacle, leading their flock to Almighty God. Fr Mervyn said Mass in Italian, which was lovely, so that everyone could understand. After the Gospel, he explained what we were doing at San Giovanni, and my situation, and then followed the Sacrament of the Sick at which I knelt before the altar, Padre Pio and Almighty God. With the prayers of the people behind me and everyone back home, I felt at peace and very relaxed. The Consecration was the supreme highlight, at one with the suffering of Christ and his Cross for the salvation of souls. To have the Marcucci family present, Antonio's mum, brother and sister (carrying child) was symbolic of the prayer of the people, those in San Giovanni, linked in communion with those back home, the family of God carrying me up Calvary, led by and supported by the shepherds, the leaders of this huge, eternal family within which I belong, ie: Frs Mark and Mervyn. Perhaps for a short while, I had the honour of being Simon of Cyrene, as Padre Pio was in a far more dramatic way as presented at the fifth station we had seen that morning.

After saying a few prayers after Mass, I went over to greet the Marcucci family with Mervyn and Mark who were already chatting away. After thanking them all at the end of a conversation with which Mark helped me a little, we went back through the old sacristy and into the larger, newer one for Fr Mark to disrobe. Then came another wonderful surprise. Fr Rinaldo had arranged for us to have tea/coffee with Fr Ermelindo.

I didn't think anything of it at the time, but once we were led through a side door from the sacristy into another room, and I saw the old friar, it dawned on me that this person knew Padre Pio. The room was full of souvenirs, mostly in English. It was like an Aladdin's cave, with photo cards of the Padre and everything from rosewood beads to snowy Padre Pio scenes. The books were all there too, so round I went scanning everything and then once Mervyn and Mark had made their introductions, I went to do the same.

We sat on chairs in the middle of the room and Fr Ermelindo told us of Padre Pio's sense of humour; for example the story of the soldier who was to meet the king and gave his response to the king's questions the wrong way round, such that he would be a soldier for twenty one years and he was two years old; also the soldier who, when he had his head scanned, they found nothing in there, and the Padre agreed 'There's nothing in there', relating a couple of jokes he used to tell. With my questions fired out we established that he did eat more than one potato a day, and that pains fluctuated in intensity. Thus, for Mark especially, Padre Pio was not a holy man removed from reality, but a holy man who could be related to, and who also possessed extraordinary blessings/graces.

Then the climax of the week arrived that Thursday afternoon. Fr Ermelindo said that he would like to bless us. He reached into the nearby drawer and pulled out a tan-coloured flattish wooden box. In it was the mitten worn by Padre Pio over his stigmatic hand and the small crucifix of his. Fr Ermelindo took the glove out of the box and blessed us all on our foreheads. Well! I was in heaven with joy and was bowled over by such an honour and privilege! The blessing was quick, but left me thrilled, excited, peaceful and happy in a way that captured my heart and overwhelmed me.

Andrew lived in hope of God's healing

Healing
12 FEBRUARY 2001

FR ERMELINDO HAD to go off to say Mass but I was eager to capture the moment on film. So off shot my coat and into position with the man who had allowed himself to be used by God in such a powerful way for the benefit of me, Mark and Mervyn. After a group photo taken by a beautiful young lady called Anna Pio, I then proceeded, having said goodbye to Fr Ermelindo, to buy up half the shop to which Anna duly totted up my account. Of course, Mark and Mervyn wouldn't allow me to carry my newly acquired piety stall, so we said our farewell to Anna. Through Mervyn I asked whether Anna was a nun, but she pointed to a silver ring on her middle finger which I presume meant that she was either engaged or married. 'Shucks,' I thought, but I guess to have Anna as my parish assistant (as housekeeper seems very politically incorrect) would not have done my spiritual journey any good at all!

We were all very much on a high, having just had Mass and experienced such a wonderful blessing. We found ourselves back in the tomb, where I just sat at the back gazing and praying in bewilderment over the graces received. I remember distinctly feeling quite well and wondered… 'Maybe I've been healed.' The prospect that a miracle may have occurred in me frightened me a bit. I slowly and tentatively passed my hand inconspicuously under my jumper as I sat bent forward in a reverent prayer-like position with my elbows on my knees. My stomach felt unusually soft and for a moment I had a bit of an adrenalin rush, 'Where was my cancer?' All of a sudden I straightened up slightly and felt again, pushing my hand further into my tummy, feeling as if I might have won the lottery and double checking the numbers on my ticket. The action was quick and feeling fleeting, because no, the cancer was still there, but perhaps a little smaller. There was disappointment, mixed with a ridiculous sense of relief that it was still there. The whole checking episode lasted a fraction of a second, and I was quickly back into my praying/gazing, made with a spirit of contentment and much consolation. To have suffering in illness was a gift. It had brought me to Padre Pio in which it found purpose and meaning, which filled me with joy, perhaps especially because at that moment I wasn't in pain, but enjoying the fruits of the suffering of the last six months and the prayers of my family in Christ.

Fr Mervyn, on my left, asked as I looked over after about fifteen minutes, what I want to do next? I said I'd like to pray the rosary at the cross under which Padre Pio received the stigmata. I also needed to purchase another ten postcards to go with the sixty I had already bought.[†] On our way round to the cross, we passed the piety stall and I bought the cards and then proceeded to enter the choir loft above the old church where the crucifix could be seen.

All three of us sat on the steps in the middle of the choir loft at the rear pew and looked up to the cross directly in front of us. Above the crucifix, which looks particularly violent, was a painting on the roof of the church of St Michael the Archangel, which drew together in a prayerful setting both St Michael's shrine and Padre Pio's home. We prayed in thanksgiving, for the sick, for our families and for our wider family who were praying for us. We managed four decades of the Joyful Mysteries (Thursday) before being turfed out by a steward, as that part of the church tour route was being closed. Downstairs the old church and the large church were still open. We went into the old church, where Fr Mark blessed my newly acquired prayer cards and we said the final decade of the rosary.

† see Appendix 2

From there we entered the large church in time for Vespers. At the end of Vespers, Fr Mervyn went up to the altar to thank Fr Rinaldo. I followed with Mark in tow. At the end of our vote of immense gratitude for what he had done for us, I asked for a photo of him. He led us into the newer sacristy and to my amazement we had a group photo in there taken by another pretty young lady, of which there seemed to be a rather plentiful supply around the church. It was uplifting to see young, as well as old, from ordinary walks of life living a life of faith and commitment to the cause of the mission at San Giovanni Rotondo.

Thus we left on cloud nine. We went back to our accommodation, where Mervyn and Mark embarked on and completed gallantly the task of sticking stamps on seventy-three postcards, while I addressed about three-quarters of them. Then we went for our final meal in yet another different, but local, restaurant called Biffo's. I had my favourite meal of the week there, including a lovely simple tomato pasta, followed by swordfish and vegetables, magnifico!! The restaurant owner put some beautiful opera on and also English pop music. Then towards the end of the meal Mervyn asked me the question, 'What has been the best part of the pilgrimage for you?' I replied after a moment of contemplation, 'The presence of God who has been so

Andrew with his parents on his graduation. July 2000

Fr Jonathan Veasey and Andrew

Frs Mervyn Tower and Mark Crisp picnicing in San Damiano, Feb '01

Andrew Robinson next to Padre Pio's chair

Andrew's intake year at Oscott September '97

Christmas 2000, Archbishop Vincent Nichols with Clive, Maria,
Andrew and Stella Robinson

James Mealey, Andrew and Matthew Jakes

Fr Harry Curtis, Andrew and Fr Jonathan Veasey

Andrew and Richard Robinson with Mgr Thomas Gavin

Kate Calnan from St Thomas More, Kidlington

Maggie Calnan from St Thomas More, Kidlington

Lourdes, October 2000. Top row (L to R) Fr Eamon Corduff, Chris O' Kane,
Andrew, Rachel Thompson, Clare Nollett, Robert Thompson,
2nd row (L to R) Doreen Robinson (Nana), Tom Bracken, Katy Hogg, Maria,
Andrew Colby, John Bentley, Stella, Clive, Richard, Bottom row (L to R)
Greg McGuire, Debbie Middleton, Baby Nathaniel, Paul Middleton.

Fr Mark Crisp, Antonio Lucia, Fr Mervyn Tower,
Mr and Mrs Marcucci in San Giovanni Rotondo.

Andrew. Early 90s   Andrew with Kath Ryan (Physio)

A family meal (L to R) Willaim Horton (Grandpa), Andrew,
Clive, Maria, Richard and Stella.

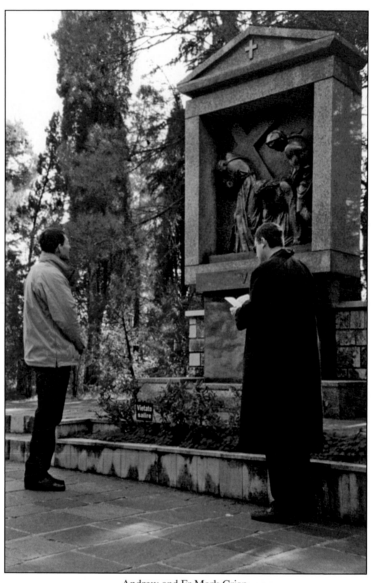

Andrew and Fr Mark Crisp.
Stations of the Cross in San Giovanni

Frs Mark, Mervyn, and Pat Kilgarriff with Andrew at Palazzola

Andrew, John, Maria and Tom (now Maria's husband)

On the plane to San Giovanni

Beatrice Upham with Andrew

Fr Ermelindo and Andrew

The plaque at Oscott

Fr Mervyn, Fr Rinaldo, Andrew, Fr Mark Crisp at St Michael's Grotto

Andrew's Spiritual Director at Oscott, Fr Hugh Sinclair

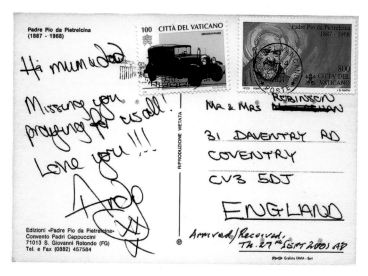

The postcard Andrew sent to his parents whist in San Giovanni and arrived
5 months to the day of his death, Sept 27, 2001

To my Mum and Dad from Andy.
(Received from Heaven Th.27th.September 2001 A.D.)

Mgr Mark Crisp and the 9am choir of St Thomas More Parish,
Coventry recording Psalm 29

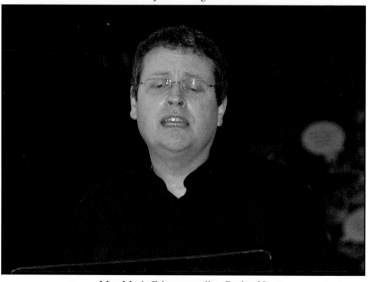

Mgr Mark Crisp recording Psalm 29

The choir of St Thomas More Parish, Coventry recording Psalm 29

The choir of St Thomas More Parish, Coventry recording Psalm 29

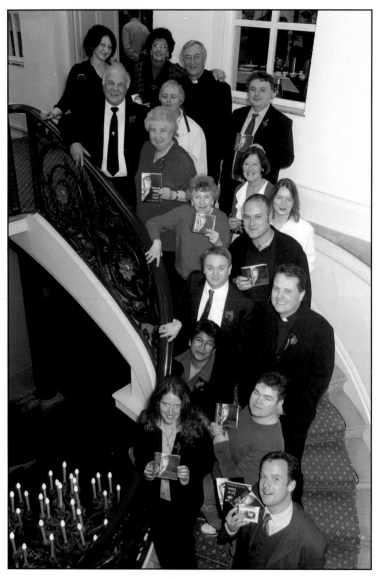

Book launch of the first edition of Tears at Night, Joy at Dawn,
March 17, 2003

apparent during the whole of our journey.' In replying to this, Fr Mervyn became very emotional, particularly as he recalled the way that love from the parish had been bestowed upon us. Mark also was somewhat choked. As much as I felt inside very emotional, unfortunately my control mechanism prevented me from crying. But I think both Mark and Mervyn recognised the extent to which I had been touched by the day's events.

We embarked on a passionate discussion during which we recognised more fully the value of the Cross in each person's life. We acknowledged, too, that we as priests (well, obviously me as training) needed to provide the key by which others can find meaning and thus joy in suffering whilst at the same time recognising the crushing effect of the cross on some, and the need for the Church to support and help each other with any cross which we may be granted during our life. To see the call to love in suffering and sacrifice for the salvation of souls as an offering to Almighty God in union with the Cross of Christ was something which Padre Pio helped us to experience and understand more fully, whilst recognising that suffering is also a mystery requiring faith, hope and trust in God.

Is Anyone Listening?

8 MARCH 2001

BACK HOME IN England, I am sitting in bed recovering from tiredness. Unfortunately, Katy isn't very well so I cannot go shopping with her to get her a birthday present this morning. God, in his providence and mercy, has given me this opportunity to have a lie-in. Physical tiredness can be such a hindrance, but at least it gives time for quiet and reflection. Prayer, thankfully, isn't only reserved for tired moments: if it were it might amount to half a Hail Mary a night as my head hits the pillow.

Since coming back from San Giovanni Rotondo life has been busy. February 21st was Cardinal Newman's two-hundredth anniversary, during which I was to preach. On one of my walks round the park I felt that I should speak about prayer, but the finished product didn't come straight to mind. God made me struggle a bit to think through truth in a way which others could relate to when dealing with problems of what we perceive as unanswered prayer.

Then there was little Megan's funeral: the school reunion; Caroline's house packing, although I just talked and made tea whilst Kathleen cleaned the kitchen and Caroline chased the stray cat in and out of the house; lectures at Oscott on Tuesdays; retreat day at Archbishop Ilsley's Secondary School; house Mass at Beatrice's. Sadly, Ann Fellows, who I visited a couple of times since coming back from San Giovanni, died a few weeks ago. Last Friday I felt an urgency to see Richard, who I know was very unwell at a hospice in Solihull. Amazingly, I glimpsed Warren Pearl Hospice in the dark on the Warwick Road that Friday night. I met his dad Eugene, Karl and Mandy and we chatted for a couple of hours. I left at 11.30pm and Richard went to his well-deserved eternal reward at 4.00am the following morning, after ten years of suffering. To think both Ann and Richard were up and about before Christmas!

Two days ago, John Bentley and I did the rosary in the grounds at Oscott. At the second sorrowful mystery, John said, 'We pray for the sick, do you want to mention anyone, Andy?' I said, 'I could, but they've all died.' John, who knew Richard as well, turned round and said, 'Is anyone listening?!' We both laughed and then continued praying confident that God knew best and that our prayers kept us close to him.

On 26 February I had my scan results. They were what I had hoped and anticipated. No change in the tumour since last time, which meant a break from treatment – PRAISE GOD! I hadn't got time for treatment, I thought. This weekend is a Maltfriscan retreat and Mass at Coventry Cathedral for Our Lady of Coventry, and Katy's birthday, as one example. I also have to go to see my friends at Abbey Hulton in Stoke on Trent and I have been wanting to speak to them to thank them for their prayers for ages. I feel God is using me and my situation, but perhaps I am packing too much in, and not trusting in God to allow me to go steady.

For example, yesterday I got up early and produced a display with my photos of San Giovanni for the parish of St Thomas More and St Hugh of Lincoln in Kidlington, thinking that Mervyn was coming up that afternoon. We had got our wires crossed. He was expecting me to go there! Now I won't have to get the display over until next week and all that rushing. Paul Edwards and Andy Franklin were kind enough to come up that afternoon, but it didn't take them long to notice that I didn't have much to give them. After a pleasant hour they were kind enough and sensitive enough to let me rest and they told me to take it easy. 'Knock three days out of your diary a week,' Paul said.

That evening I was up at church for the rosary, Mass, which was said for me, and a talk by Brother Stanley of the

Philippines. He spoke about his experience of God. He was a father of thirteen and became very ill, coughing blood. He was on a life support machine. They asked his wife for permission to turn it off, but she told them to keep it on. After three days, he suddenly got out of bed. He explained what happened during those three days. He saw a bright light, a figure which he recognised as Jesus with swirling clouds over his head. The cloud came down and he saw a video of his life. His life progressed before him, but sins were shown in slow motion. Afterwards Jesus told him to proclaim to the world about his Divine Mercy. 'Why choose me?' Brother Stanley asked. 'The beauty of my Divine Mercy can only be seen by those who know the misery of sin.' He was reunited with his body which was flashed on the monitor. Only the life support machine kept him alive. On returning to his body he removed his oxygen mask and the tube down his throat and got up. The nurse by this time had legged it in shock.

What was encouraging for me was not so much the miracle, but what he said afterwards. He reiterated the truths I knew in my heart. The fact that there is no sin too big for God to forgive, except one – not to accept God's forgiveness, or not to believe that God can forgive you. He also stressed the importance of confession. He said the shame/weight of those sins he had confessed had been lessened. Padre Pio was forever in the confessional. He also said that for any soul you save, you save your own. In other words, if we allow God to work through us such that he is able to touch the heart of another, we are allowing God to save our own soul also. We have a free will to choose God and love or not to choose him and love. We are, therefore, instrumental in God's saving of us and of others.

Brother Stanley was united to the Church. He did not lay on hands for healing because the Church had not authorised him to. Yet the Church encouraged him to evangelise as his mission from God called him to. The miracle of his cure is being painstakingly investigated by the Church.

There then followed reverence to the Divine Mercy and a large picture of the Divine Mercy was venerated in procession in honour and thanksgiving of the mercy and compassion of God.

Finally, how do we witness in our western world? Brother Stanley said by the way we live our lives and our actions.

The Divine Mercy

Getting Right with God

17 MARCH 2001

YET ANOTHER BUSY WEEK, although I have had to slow down over the last couple of days. First there was a practice for the choir for the Mass on Sunday for Our Lady of Coventry. Then it was off to Leigh-Ann's thirtieth birthday party. I'd been shopping with Katy that morning for Greg's and Katy's present (Greg – Leigh-Ann's partner. I've known him for years and it was his birthday, too). So I had got Katy some pyjamas she had wanted and Greg a T-shirt reduced from £20 to £6 – not bad!! At the party I had a good chat with Rosemary – Greg's mum, who has a pace-maker and has also had to stare death in the face. But amongst the tears we had some laughs and a gentle dance to the not-so-gentle disco music.

After chatting to Mike, Dan, Fay, Greg, Leigh-Ann, Andy, Marie-Ann, Doug, Betty, Sarah, Patsy and Lillian, I got home at midnight, knackered. In bed that night I remember feeling concerned that I didn't share in people's tears by crying myself. Was I too hard, too 'in control' to be sensitive? I didn't seem to think so, but I was not so sure.

Saturday – off to Stratford for the Maltfriscan retreat, after spending an hour at Greg's to collect my belated Christmas present. *Star Wars* framed picture, of course! It was good to chat with Mandy who was holding herself together well after Richard's death. Back home, I baked a cake for Katy's 24th birthday the following day. Sunday was a wonderful day – the celebration of Our Lady of Coventry at Coventry Cathedral and Katy's birthday at Frankie and Bennie's Restaurant that night were both highly successful. And my cake, complete with diabolical toffee icing, went down a treat. The toffee dressing was supposed to spell Katy with the 't' shaped as a girl, but it went all over the shop. However, we had a lot of laughs over it, and over Debbie and Katy's success in chatting up two fellas at the bar resulting in the donation of another jug of pink cocktail!!

On Monday, 12th I worked on the Internet to find *The Common Good* and other encyclicals for my 'Social Ethics' course. Tuesday – Oscott, plus a meal with Andy and Johnny in the evening. Wednesday was Richard's funeral which was both beautifully simple and special just like Richard. Mandy was upset and Karl, too, though he seemed to cope by immersing himself in the Bible, unable to engage with Richard's family and friends at all. Johnny B had broken his leg by playing footy that Monday, so I picked him up in the car along with Mike Green, went to the funeral, then the cemetery, back to Oscott to drop Mike G off (he was refereeing the North Staffs School Championship Football at Oscott). Back to the reception, a good chat with Eugene (Richard's dad), Dave Kemp (his friend), back to Oscott to drop John Bentley off, back to Coventry in time for Fr Mervyn to pick me up to take me back to Birmingham for a meal with Fr Mark at Kath Ryan's that evening.

By Thursday I was a wreck, in pain, and didn't start coming round until Saturday (today). This morning I went swimming with Mum at *The Village* hotel. The first time I had been swimming for 14 months. I was anxious and slow with the 'old dears' passing me on both sides like Ian Thorpe (Australian Olympic swimming champion called 'the Torpedo'). But I felt OK, praise God.

However, I feel the cancer is perhaps growing somewhat. I had a blood test on Friday and suspect I could be due for further treatment soon, but I would so love to go to Abbey Hulton this weekend to thank all the parishioners up there for their prayers. *Please Lord, I hope that this will be possible and that by your grace I will be able to encourage them in faith, love and trust in you. Amen.*

Last Tuesday, whilst at Oscott, I had spiritual direction with Fr Hugh – it was a very blessed time. I had pretty well decided a few days previous to have a long confession as if it were my last. A number of occasions led me to this definite decision.

Firstly, Padre Pio spent much of his life hearing confessions. The importance of confessing all in sincerity and humility and shame was and is crucial on the journey of the soul to God. In the video on Padre Pio called *Hope, Trust and Pray* (I think) a man (with a wonderful authentic voice from the Northern working-class coalface it seemed) recounted a confession he had with Padre Pio. After confessing his sins, Padre Pio said, 'You've left out something.' 'I can't think what it is, Father,' came the reply. 'The woman in the park.' 'It all came flooding back to me,' said the man, 'Oh yes, Father.' 'You've been carrying that sin around with you since 1941,' said Padre Pio. 'There's something else you've forgotten,' said Padre Pio. 'No Father, honestly I cannot think of anything else.' 'Your rosary beads, give them to me.' The man gave Padre Pio his rosary beads and then Padre Pio blessed them and gave them back to the grateful and relieved man! What a beautiful encounter, I thought, and the freedom that man must have felt knowing that, in his humility, God's mercy was upon him and that he was at rights with God.

Secondly, Bro Stanley's witness and proclamation of God's Divine Mercy and his pointing to the Sacrament of Confession.

Thirdly, seeing Richard and Ann in particular, I realised I did not want to wait any longer before making my final confession. I wanted my next confession to be as if it were my final confession, wheeling out sins of the past and their cumulative effect on my life. I didn't want to wait until I was only half conscious before making my most sincere 'life-time' confession. Although, I haven't had sexual intercourse, I am very far from pure in that respect. It was this aspect of my life which had prevented me entering for the priesthood at a much earlier age. At least, it was probably the most prominent factor. God didn't reject me or fail to use me until I finally entered seminary – of course not – but if his will was for me to go into priesthood much earlier, my will was taking me along a different path from the one he intended (as a result of my selfishness and human desires)! I know I had already confessed most, if not all of these sins before, but I wanted to lay all my sinful cards on the table and their cumulative effects. Perhaps I had missed one or two of them out. But in front of God and his servant, Fr Hugh, I lay my sins before all and then saw the table to be wiped clean by God's mercy just like that. Fr Hugh in his wisdom and humility presented words of encouragement and faith and after absolution I went away – a free man!!

A Roller Coaster Ride

30 MARCH 2001

YET MORE TWISTS and turns in God's perfect plan for me. I tell you, this perfect plan is a real roller-coaster. Unfortunately for me at the moment, it is the kind of roller-coaster you want to get off! However, my consolation as always is that God is very much with me, like the strong and sturdy safety bar that holds you in and stops you being tossed out into the abyss. God comes to me in my calmness and in the many people who have visited me and who are praying for me. I feel his protection all around me, but even so, I will still be glad when this ride is over. I think I would prefer to try that kiddies' train ride next, in order to get my breath back. So what's been happening?

Last week I went to College (Oscott) on Monday and stayed overnight and all day Tuesday. I went to the Maltfriscan meeting on Tuesday night and celebrated John's and Mandy's birthdays. Wednesday to Friday was spent preparing for the weekend, resting and thinking of what to say in relation to the prodigal son. Friday night was the Oscott play *Rope* which was brilliant and Thursday morning I managed to go swimming again.

However, on Thursday I didn't go to the toilet, neither on Friday, so by Saturday morning I knew that there was something wrong, especially as I didn't feel constipated. I decided I would still go to Abbey Hulton to visit my old parish of Our Lady and St Benedict's and everything went very well, in spite of the really severe stomach cramp and badly diminishing appetite. By Sunday night at *The Plough* where we celebrated Mums' Day, I barely picked at the smoked haddock. Monday I knew I was in trouble, but I felt a deep sense of peace that I had completed my mission to Abbey Hulton.

I had no further pressing engagements and it was as if I could now let my body have its own way – and it did! I distinctly remember telling Katy on Sunday night that I felt I had a blockage from the tumour in the bowel and that I would have to wear a 'bag' but that I felt a peace knowing that I had finished my personal commitments, which I felt encouraged to undertake by my conscience within and that God was very much with me.

To cut a long story short, on Monday, Katy and Maureen looked after me. Maureen (retired ex-nurse – very spiritual, prayerful person) felt I had constipation, even though the enemas did not shift much. By the evening I was in the Q.E. and after being told by the doctor after an X-ray that I had constipation, I proceeded to explain why I thought the tumour was blocking my bowel. He went and took a closer look at the X-rays and came back to confirm that I was right. I stayed overnight in the admissions ward, which was noisier than Piccadilly Circus in the rush hour, with bleeps, bells, buzzers going off all the time. So I stayed all of Tuesday, which I spent in the ward with Mum and Dad until 6.00 pm at which point we left the hospital so that I could rest at home. We had waited for the doctor all day.

The diaconate ordination of Andrew's year in the
Chapel at Oscott College, Birmingham.

Ordination Hopes
31 MARCH 2001

IT IS HARD, you know, coming to terms with dying. I felt, perhaps for the first time since I was diagnosed with cancer, a kind of numbness at the prospect of it being perhaps somewhat closer than I had thought. The treatment so far had been a relative success but the blocked bowel was a hiccup, and yesterday things were starting to go wrong.

I was due to have a 'stent pipe' fitted between the tumour in the bowel causing the blockage and the bowel wall. This stent pipe, once fitted, opens out (ie the diameter is increased) to allow the waste to go through it. However, despite the optimism of two doctors, the procedure failed. The blockage was too tight to get the line through, and so the pipe couldn't follow the wire into position. Unusually and unfortunately, I made the mistake of allowing the doctors' optimism to increase my hopes that the situation would soon be rectified. I had not prepared myself enough for the prospect of an operation proper were the stent pipe procedure to fail (the latter being a relatively unobtrusive procedure done via the rectum without the need for knives, wounds, openings and anaesthetics).

Thus after the two hours of prodding up my rear end (for want of a better expression) I was not only confronted with the prospect of an operation, but worse still, I had had my hopes dashed and Mum was upset and crying.

For the first time I had not braced myself for a negative outcome and so for the first time I felt true disappointment. At my stage of cancer, an operation is not good and often signifies that you are on the slippery slope to the bottom, and that the slope ain't that long! For the first time, I had to hide true disappointment. It wasn't easy with Mum weeping over me, but I hope I managed it. Fortunately, only Mum and Dad came to see me that day, and so I didn't have to sustain the positive act for long. Once they had gone I breathed a sigh of relief. Now I could deal with my own disappointment in the silence and solitude of my own room. I cannot show the disappointment, or at least I don't want to, not because it is wrong, but because I do not want it to appear as though my faith and trust in God is waning.

You see, the day before the stent pipe procedure (Thursday) I was very honoured by a visit from His Grace, Archbishop Vincent Nichols. Not only did he ask how things were, but he said that he felt we could talk about ordination, and more or less said that he would go along with it if I desired to be ordained. I was excited, stunned a bit that I was being told this in my dressing-gown by the Archbishop standing at the back of my bed while the nurses made my bed. It was all quite bizarre. I said that perhaps we could talk about it after the current blockage was sorted out. My mind thought of the where, when, and hows of a possible ordination after the Archbishop had left.

I had a number of visitors that day, and I was quite upbeat. 'I'll be getting better 'cos God wants me to be ordained,' I thought subconsciously. Everything's in hand. So, of course, when the stent pipe procedure failed, I became somewhat confused and disappointed. I still had trust and faith, but when I felt I had an idea of the short-medium-term plan, all of a sudden I had no idea at all, and I must be honest, in the quiet of my room, my heart sank in between inner cries of 'What's going on,' and 'Crumbs, I could die a lot sooner that I thought'. My consolation was a very funny episode of *They Think It's All Over* on TV where they picked the best moments of previous episodes. My other consolation was, of course, the knowledge of many, many prayers and that God must know what he's doing.

By the following morning I had regained my inner calmness somewhat. I am starting to think of dying with relative peace and trust in God again. I need to try and get through this operation as best I can, and God's will regarding ordination will reveal itself in due course. Mum has been upset again today and I've given her a few reassuring hugs and cuddles. It is so very hard for Mum, who gets her hopes up all the time and finds it hard to face the reality of my dying as a strong possibility. Today, I feel she has gone some way towards it and God, in his mercy, will carry us through stage by stage, hour by hour, day by day. It is not for me to know the plan, but rather to trust in God's love for me and my family. What is important to me is that I remain in him and in so doing be an instrument by which God draws his people to himself, both in my living and my faithfulness in dying – whatever is to come.

Lord, that I may grow in the gift of your Spirit – in patience, faith, love, kindness, humility and trust (etc) that others may know that you are alive in me. I am sorry for my selfishness and desire to be in control myself, rather than allow my will to be your will. Please forgive me, Lord, and sustain me in your merciful love. Amen.

Mum said today that someone put it to her that others who are in my position and who do not get cured or have their prayers answered may lose heart and faith. A miracle for me must be seen as favouritism and that God prefers some more than others. That the prayers of some are better than others. Therefore, maybe I am not to be cured physically, but rather to lead people to trust and to seek first the inner peace of God and unite with him and not so much long for life, holidays and full bellies, etc., in this life/world.

People are all praying hard for me at the moment. At Mass today, little James said he prays for me every day. 'He's my best friend, he is!' as he went around collecting the hymn books. James is ten to eleven and I met him when I went to Elizabeth Milewski's year 6 class at St Thomas More. When I asked the children, 'What do you want to do when you get older?' (after thanking them for their prayers, etc.) young James proclaimed he wanted to be a priest. Such a kind, loving and generous-notioned child, I hope he gets to be one!

Went to see Professor David Kerr today at the Q.E. He was very good and he explained that the 'bag' operation might not be possible if the cancer, which acts like a glue, prevents the surgeon finding a bit of healthy bowel to draw from.

In myself, I feel much better than I did after the stent pipe procedure. Things are looking a little bleaker all the time, but at the moment I feel quite mentally and spiritually OK, thank God and everyone's prayers. Had a relaxing chat with Grandpop in the conservatory.

The newly ordained Deacons from Andrew's year,
with Archbishop Vincent Nichols

The Call to Priesthood
3 APRIL 2001

MARIA AND TOM have returned from their three-month 'Round the World' trip.[†] Praise God for their safe return and that my illness did not require them to return early!

When I think of my life, I think of the story of Jesus' encounter with the rich young man. I feel that I can identify strongly with him. I was a worldly rich young man with house, job, prospects, etc. I was a reasonably good Christian, trying to keep the commandments of God – going to church, supporting the youth group, the SVP-Youth, CAYA, altar-serving, music groups, saying prayers (when I could remember). But I lacked one thing – 'Go and sell everything you have, give it to the poor, and follow me' (Matt. 19:21).

The priesthood, for me, epitomised the last request, and when I first felt the call to this request of priesthood I could

† see Appendix 3

not comply, and like the rich young man (whom Jesus loved for keeping God's commandments) I went away sad.

For me it was impossible to take up this cross of priesthood because I was very rich. I had independence, security, a girlfriend and control of my own life. It was impossible for me to sacrifice these things. It wasn't so much that God asks all people to sacrifice these things, but the question is, could we do it if he did? I could and do completely know the mind of the disciples who asked Jesus, 'Well, who can be saved?' (Matt. 19-25), ie: who can seriously let go of human desires for the sake of love of God and love of neighbour? Jesus replies, 'For man it is impossible, but for God, nothing is impossible' (Matt. 19:26).

I threw myself at the mercy of God when I threw myself into Seminary College three and a half years ago. In fact, the process started eighteen months before then, when Katy recognised that there was something disturbing me. Katy recognised in me the sadness of the rich young man as he walked away. When I told her that I felt God might be calling me to the priesthood, I was explaining to Katy what I had buried within myself for ten years – the cause of my sadness. It was impossible for me to 'Go, sell everything…. and follow me' (Matt. 19:22). Five years later, BY GOD'S GRACE ALONE (everyone's prayers and my recognition of my total weakness), not only has God brought me to the priesthood, but over the course of a painful journey, he has brought me to be able to say that 'I want to be a priest, not out of a sense of duty, but out of love for him and love for my neighbour.' My heart of stone is turning towards being a heart of flesh, not by anything I have done because for me it was truly impossible, but by the grace of God.

As a result, I have come towards a peace and happiness, deep within, which I had not known and which I trust will find fulfilment and completion in the life to come. This peace, with the will of God, is the pearl of great price which, in hindsight, is worth selling everything for.

My illness has played a substantial part in my journey to God, to peace and to freedom. The journey is by no means easy, but when you come towards the light at the end of the tunnel, and you feel its warmth, you taste its peace and freedom, you hear the noise of the crowds of angels cheering you on in praise of God, who draws us to the light.

As you get closer and closer to the finish line you feel the exhilaration, you begin to smile and shed a tear of joy, one final push and you cross the line. You enter that light in all its glory… Death is that moment of transition when, please God, I will be fully reunited to the Father and enter into that peace, freedom and happiness which I have tasted in this life, because God has made that which was impossible for me, possible.

Maybe I will be ordained a priest, maybe not, but as Fr Louis McRaye said in Mass about me, 'His intention is there and that is what is important', ie: that change of heart brought about by my willingness to place myself at the feet of God's mercy and his willingness to raise me up.

'I will praise you, Lord, for you have rescued me, and not let my enemies rejoice over me. My soul sings psalms to you unceasingly, O Lord my God, I will thank you forever!' (Psalm 29)

Diary Addendum

Andrew's mother, Stella, wrote the following diary notes for 25 and 27 April – Andrew's last day.

Andrew with his mother, Stella

A Lovely Memory
25 APRIL 2001

ANDREW HAD BEEN on a liquid diet which together with his tumour and blockage resulted in him becoming quite weak.

Mervyn and Mark came to see Andrew in hospital which pleased him very much. Maria, Richard, Clive, Katy, Tom and myself were present. Mervyn had brought his oils with him and asked Andrew if he would like the Sacrament of the Sick again having had it several times before during his illness. Andrew's reply was 'yes please', so Fr Mervyn read the prayers of the sick, Fr Mark the Gospel, we all had Holy Communion, with Andrew receiving a very tiny piece of Jesus' body as he was unable to eat and only able to sip a little liquid by now.

Mervyn blessed him with the holy oils and when it was over, Andrew in his weak state asked for his breviary and stated that he would read his psalm as a testimony to his faith. It was quite a heavy task for him and the morphine made it difficult for him to focus on the words. With great determination he stiltingly read a few words, then he took up his prayer card and placed it under each line as a bookmark to help him follow the words of the psalm down the page, saying it line by line and sometimes saying a line twice. It was very difficult – the psalm he once knew and said each night with us in prayer. We listened intently to each word, for each line to be said, praying he would finish it to the end. The prayer was coming from his heart; he was willing himself to go on. At last it was finished, the book lay on his bed, we lifted it off and his head lay back on the pillow, he was exhausted. What an acknowledgement of his life and faith – God truly blessed him. Maria cried, and he turned his head and said 'My angel', and she said 'No, you're my angel'.

Clive and I stayed the night at the Q.E. Hospital and were blessed with some quiet time with Andrew, just feeling each other's love. It was hot in his room, Clive helped him to the window and he looked out at the night lights below. It was in the early hours and we made a cup of tea. Andrew sipped his drink and we drank ours in the cool corridor sitting on the chairs talking a little, praying and in silence – a lovely memory.

PSALM 29

I will praise you, Lord, you have rescued me
and have not let my enemies rejoice over me.

O Lord, I cried to you for help
and you, my God have healed me.
O Lord, you have raised my soul from the dead,
restored me to life from those who sink into the grave

Sing psalms to the Lord, you who love him,
give thanks to his holy name.
His anger lasts but a moment: his favour all through life.
At night there are tears, but joy comes with dawn.

I said to myself in my good fortune;
'Nothing will ever disturb me.'
Your favour had set me on a mountain fastness,
then you hid your face and I was put to confusion.

To you Lord, I cried, to my God I made appeal:
'What profit would my death be, my going to the grave?
Can dust give you praise or proclaim your truth?'

The Lord listened and had pity. The Lord came to my help.
For me you have changed my mourning into dancing,
you removed my sackcloth and clothed me with joy.
So my soul sings psalms to you unceasingly.
O Lord my God, I will thank you forever.

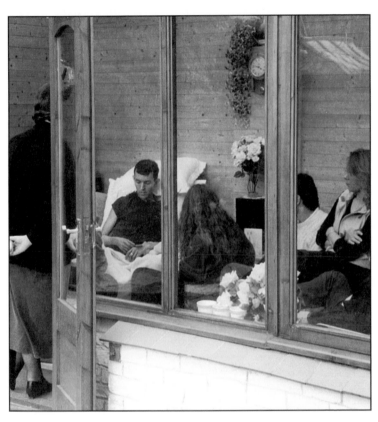

Andrew at home in the conservatory on the day he died

Andrew's Last Day

27 APRIL 2001

ON THE DAY before Andrew died he had to be washed and changed having lost control of his bowels and too weak to do it for himself. He said to me, 'I too have lost my dignity; I now know how Jesus felt at the cross when they stripped him of his garments.'

At 2pm he expected to return home, he couldn't wait, I think it was the longest night and morning of his life. He would sleep a little, then waking up he would think it was time to go home, but when 2pm came they said to Clive it could be up to 6pm. He didn't dare tell Andrew and negotiated 3pm and the ambulance men came at that time. Andrew clapped his hands and despite the pain and difficulty they moved him on a stretcher to the ambulance three floors below.

Clive told me to go in the ambulance with Andrew just in case, while he drove back. What a journey – traffic causing stopping and starting through the middle of Birmingham. Andrew was tipped to the side on some corners – they said sorry and he tried to smile as I held his hand. I had to sit on my seat with the seat belt on, it was difficult. As we motored along the A45 to Coventry we passed the high hotel building at Allesley, he clapped his hands and gave a smile, on arriving at Daventry Road, another clap of the hands – how relieved I was. It was the worst journey of my life, I didn't think he would make it, I thanked God.

All the youngsters were waiting, banners of welcome, some balloons, I just wish he had been a bit stronger to enjoy it all. Maria, Richard, Tom, Greg Maguire, Rachel and Katy were all waiting to receive him home. Clive arrived in the car at the same time as the ambulance. They were going to take him to his bedroom but he wanted to sit in the conservatory. 'That's the only room we haven't cleaned,' exclaimed Rachel in dismay! Andrew sat in his Grandmother's armchair: 'Marvellous,' he said with a smile on his face. The sun shone and the birds sang as the late afternoon gently closed on this special time together. Andrew read some of his cards and smiled at his family and friends for about twenty minutes, then they lifted him up and helped him to the blue settee in the house, where he sat for ten minutes before being ready to go to bed.

Gently we helped him put his arms round his brother Richard and Tom and Clive stood behind to make sure he was safe. We took him up the stairs to his bedroom where he was so delighted to see how lovely they had made it with decorations. Fr Mark had brought his Star Wars posters to cover the mirrors and the room was warm and cosy. He was so relieved to be in his own bed. 'What a joy' was written all over his face.

We thought we would have to do everything ourselves but an army of health workers seemed to kick in. Evelyn, a lovely nurse, arrived to sort out his tablets and morphine and to see if we needed anything. She said to ring her or the doctor if we needed anything and that two district nurses would be along in the evening. They did come and were quite cross as they had been given the wrong address. They had spent half an hour looking for us. They were not happy and one was a little sharp to him at first, but they calmed down saying as they came out of his room, 'He is very poorly'.

A night nurse came at 10pm but as we were not ready to leave Andrew yet, she had a cup of tea. At 2am she came up and said, 'You'd better get some sleep, there is another day tomorrow.' As I left, Andrew said 'Mass', so I said, 'Fr Mark is coming to say Mass at 7.30pm tomorrow night.' This settled him and he drifted off again. I didn't really want to leave his side. Eileen, our night nurse, was from Sacred Heart parish. When she realised who Andrew was, she turned to Clive and said, 'It is a privilege to be here.' Eileen was part of a prayer group who had been praying for Andrew.

At about 4.30 am Clive got up and the nurse said to him, 'Andrew's breathing has changed, you might like to be with him just in case'. We all quietly came into his bedroom. Maria telephoned Fr Mark who came over from Oscott and prepared Mass earlier than we had planned. Clive phoned Monsignor Thomas Gavin, our parish priest, and he must have moved like grease lightening because despite his age and his crutches he was on the doorstep in half an hour with Fr Jonathan Veasey.

With all three priests present, we celebrated our last Holy Mass together at 5.30 in the morning. We sang hymns and he opened his eyes, saw the priests and the altar and whispered 'Amen' in the right places, happy and content that he was having Mass. When Eileen, a nursing assistant from Social Services, left she said, 'It has been a pleasure and a joy to have been with Andrew'.

Through the day he opened his eyes a little: he was in pain, but knew we were there, contractions lasting about thirty to forty-five seconds at fifteen-minute intervals. Evelyn arrived, saw he was in pain and put his morphine up from forty-five to sixty milligrams. (Clive was worried but she explained that it was to relieve the pain and that her faith would not let her do any harm to him, and then he trusted her.)

† see Appendix 4

Our doctor arrived, Dr Madu Garala. He spoke to Andrew who knew he was there and gave a half smile. He asked if we minded if he said a prayer with him, to which we said, please do. He prayed with Andrew in silence for a while, told us he could not do anything for him and said goodbye to him. My sister-in-law, Clare Nollett, said later that he looked a kindly doctor and that she could see his distress at knowing there was nothing he could do. He said it was wonderful to see the whole family praying, it was very rare and reassuring. He is a Hindu and a lovely doctor.

All the family and the wider family, our parents, brothers and sisters and his uncle and aunties, prayed the rosary and sang hymns, finishing with a couple of Maltfriscan songs, sung by Fr Mark, Maria and Katy, the last one being 'Beautiful Lady'.† Andrew opened his eyes and was smiling, and just seemed to stop breathing, a little blood trickled from the corner of his mouth. My brother put some tissue under his chin. They stopped singing, thinking he had died and he started breathing again, and they started singing from where they had stopped. His smile remained and he stopped breathing again just before the end of the hymn as if he just wanted to wait until they had finished the hymn.

A short time later Archbishop Vincent came. It was very sad that he had missed his living presence but we were happy and blessed that he was there.

† see Appendix 4

ANDREW CLIVE (ANTHONY) ROBINSON
Born 23rd June 1969 A.D.
Born into heaven. 27th April. 2001 A.D.

Beloved son of Clive & Stella.
Brother of Maria & Richard.
✝
Grandson of Doreen & Jack Robinson.(d.)
& William & Edna Horton (d).

Faithful Christian witness to all.
Active parishioner of St.Thomas More Church.
4th. Year. Seminarian of Oscott College.
Greatly loved & missed by all family & friends.
God bless you always.

"Let us pray for each other
until we meet merrily in heaven."

Andrew died on 27 April 2001 and is buried in
Canley Cemetery, Coventry

Special Thanks

8 MAY 2001

The words of Andrew's father, Clive,
given at the end of the funeral Mass.

'ON BEHALF OF OUR SON, Andrew, Maria and Richard, Mum and Pop and Stella and myself, I want to thank you all: Andrew's friends from work, all his friends from Oscott and other walks of life, friends and work colleagues of Stella and myself, our own family, our brothers and sisters from other churches, neighbours, all Andrew's friends from other parishes and our very own parishioners here in St Thomas More, indeed everyone for all the love, compassion, caring and prayers you have all shown to my family.

Every compassionate thought, every tear and every act of kindness is a prayer and an act of love no matter who it is from and no matter what your belief, they are all most surely, for our family, an experience of God's kingdom and the hallowing of his name.

I think we must be the most supported and cared for grieving family there has ever been. We are so uplifted and supported by you all that Andrew has moved not only straight into heaven but even more deeply and mystically into our hearts and minds. God is being so gentle with us through the love you have for Andrew and our family. The way our whole parish and others have worked together to make last night and today the magnificent celebration of Andrew's life and faith that it is, is an act of love and unity which is exactly what Andrew wants. You have gladdened our hearts and filled us with hope.

For Stella and myself, our one and in an ultimate sense, our only prayer, that we have always asked of God, is that all our three children will keep their faith, love and serve God in this life and be with him in the next. Today, together as the children of God, we have witnessed to completion the honouring of this prayer by almighty God for our first born son, Andrew. Our precious son has been on loan to us for 31 years and it has been a great privilege and joy to be his parents. I think I have a little understanding of the Jewish custom of offering their first born son to the Lord.

In many ways it seems as though God through Andrew has united the whole of our Birmingham diocese through our Cardinal Newman prayer. It actually feels as though we are one family with living examples like Kidlington and Abbey Hulton where Andrew was on placement for just a few weeks, and many other communities. This unity has of course a very loving and caring shepherd in our Archbishop, who I am going to call 'Fr Vincent' because the warmth and love we have experienced from him makes his official titles, of which he is truly worthy, too distant at this time.

This special oneness and unity my family is experiencing of our Catholic Church, is epitomised in our very special parish priest, 'Monsignor' (Thomas Gavin). Another title perhaps, but one which carries with it tremendous mutual love and affection. The speed with which he came to our house at 5am on Friday morning, and the sheer determination with which he climbed our stairs to be at Andrew's side in his hour of need, despite his crutches and painful knees, says so much about this wonderful wise and magnificent servant of the Lord. Once again he brings that special perceptive balance of respect, dignity and love to all our sacramental occasions. He is indeed a permanent member of God's 'First Team' who will never be relegated! Fathers Jonathan, Mark, Mervyn and Hugh Sinclair, Andrew's spiritual director, Deacon Pat and Tony, Maureen and Kath… there are just so many of you that have been there for Andrew and us. Stella and I are overwhelmed with gratitude to you all.

So many prayers have been said that I can say to you with absolute certainty, that none of those prayers are wasted and that what has happened together with Andrew's willing consent, his 'Yes' to God, is God's will.

The most well known 'Yes' to God is that of our Blessed Lady. Without her 'Yes' to God we would have nothing. Through her 'Yes' to God we have everything. The reason for it all is, 'because we are so resistant to God'. To which today is a wonderful exception. Redemptive suffering willingly offered up in love to our Lord overcomes this resistance. Andrew had trodden this path, committing himself daily to giving his life to God, and is now safely in the arms of our Lord and praying for the rest of us.

Sometimes we feel strong in our faith, sometimes we are hanging on by our fingernails and sometimes we try to carry everything on our own, but we are all here today because of Andrew. If one soul is saved through knowing Andrew, he would say to me, 'It was worth it, Dad'. If just one person, one soul says, 'Yes' to God through knowing Andrew, then his eyes will shine with joy and we will see the biggest smile on his face you have ever seen.

Thank you, all of you, including those here in spirit, for your love and being here for us.'

PRAYER FOR CANONIZATION
OF CARDINAL JOHN HENRY NEWMAN
(Beatified on September 19th, 2010)

The prayer that was used by people of the diocese during Andrew's illness.

Eternal Father, you led John Henry Newman to follow the kindly light of Truth, and he obediently responded to your heavenly calls at any cost. As writer, preacher, counsellor and educator, as pastor, Oratorian, and servant of the poor he laboured to build up your Kingdom.

Grant that through your Vicar on Earth we may hear the words, 'Well done, thou good and faithful servant, enter into the company of the canonized saints'.

May you manifest your Servant's power of intercession by even extraordinary answers to the prayers of the faithful throughout the world. We pray particularly for our intentions in his name and in the name of Jesus Christ your Son our Lord. Amen.

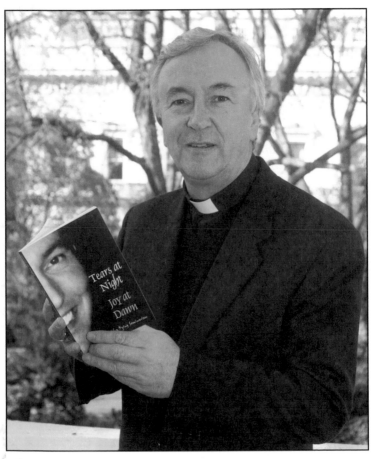

Archbishop Vincent Nichols at the launch of
Tears at Night, Joy at Dawn, March 17, 2003.

Letters

DURING HIS LIFE ANDREW gave encouragement to many. In his last months, his prayerfulness, his cheerfulness and the way in which he spoke about sharing in the cross of Christ inspired and moved many more.

Archbishop Vincent invited people to write to him if they had a treasured memory of Andrew or if on reading his journal something they had read had struck a chord, moved or encouraged them in some way.

Archbishop Vincent's post bag increased significantly over the years as many people around the world responded to his request.

Here are a selection of these letters which share so eloquently and beautifully the impact that reading Andrew's journal had on them.

I HAVE RECENTLY FINISHED reading *Tears at Night, Joy at Dawn* and it was fantastic. I think it is the best book I have ever read, and I have read lots of book.

Andrew was clearly a remarkable man and you're really lucky to have known him. I know this wasn't the point Andrew was trying to make with his words but what really moved me was the way he lived his life. He enjoyed Mass, praying, kindness, trying to be selfless, and wasn't afraid, he didn't live hiding the person he was. His words have made me have a look at my own life and realise how awful it is. Father I'm sure you are aware of the world that we live in. I, like most young people, am selfish, unkind, unforgiving, and most importantly do not give God much thought. When I was a kid we're all taught about how important we are, given everything and told to be the best, to get on in life. I'm positive our parents never meant it that way but us young people, myself included, are so full of our own self-importance, we don't know the meaning of living without or waiting because we get everything on credit and everything is instant. Life is so fast paced we never find a minute to stop and think. But Andrew's words have opened my eyes Father. He really made God the centre of his life and found peace so easily. He made me realise how easy it is to love God and how unhappy my life is. I truly believed that by having everything I was already in heaven but now

I see I was a step away from winding a noose around my neck.

Andrew tells us he hadn't had sexual intercourse and I found this totally surprising because he'd had a girlfriend, Katy, and was attractive but he felt so comfortable living the way God wanted him to.

His innocence is brilliant and inspiring. Us young people have all gone a bit mad with our lifestyles and older people encourage us with words like 'go and have fun' and 'enjoy yourself you only live once'. But Andrew said no that's not how he wanted to live and I've realised it's not how I want to live. Andrew's example has made me so comfortable changing my life and I'm living a simpler and, what most people would think, boring lifestyle but I am so much happier. In loving God you can properly find yourself. I don't like what I see in myself but at least now I can see it. I've become less selfish, more respectful of others, and have a lot more respect for myself. I've started going to Mass, praying and have even been to confession which was the most humiliating and hardest thing I've ever done but I might give it another try at some point.

I believe the Church has so much to offer the world but could concentrate more on young adults. If more of us could realise how happy we can be letting go of the things we are obsessed with and think are so important. Why must we always want the best clothes and cars etc? Why are we so interested in having fun, sex, drinking, drugs, etc? We let the world influence us and I don't think most young people realise how false it all is and that we have a choice.

I've found living simpler and trying to love God so much easier than my crazy lifestyle and I'm so much happier. I didn't realise how easy it was to love God and I don't think most young people do. Andrew's words show us how easy it can be and should be.

God is truly amazing and we all are quite pathetic and unworthy of his love but we have it nonetheless and should be eternally grateful. I know I'm still an awful person and have a long journey ahead of me but I feel God's presence in my life and feel happy that even though I may never be as strong and as good a person as Andrew was, God will understand that I'm trying.

Thank you so much Father for reading my letter and keep me in mind in your next prayer.

Pamela Santangeli, Glasgow

~

MY NAME IS EILEEN GIBNEY the night nurse mentioned in the diary of Andrew Robinson.

Your Grace, we all had been praying for Andrew for such a long time during our celebrations of Mass and in our little prayer group. When I was given the referral to go to Andrew and his family I felt very honoured. All my patients are special to me as my work specifically involves palliative care. When someone is so close to death God is so close by, so for me it is always a privilege.

During that short time I spent with Andrew and his family my life has been touched (9 hours) in a very special way. I felt a serene and vibrant presence of love and the Holy Spirit, it was a truly moving and inspirational experience. To have shared at the table of the Lord with Andrew at his last Mass in this life was also a very humbling experience.

Eileen & Kevin Gibney, Coventry

~

I HAVE JUST FINISHED READING 'Tears at Night Joy at Dawn' by Andrew Robinson. I bought the book in Lewisham, South London, only yesterday.

Now I am sitting on a coach on my journey home to Belfast and for most of the journey I have been re-reading Andrew's book. I cannot remember a time when I have cried or rather had tears flowing from my eyes in such abundance.

In February I was staying at Quarr Abbey on the Isle of Wight and met there three seminarians from Oscott. One of them, James a deacon, is to be ordained a priest this year. These three young men showed me much care and love while I was in great inward turmoil. It was at Quarr that I finally accepted the need for me to 'come home' and seek to be received into the Church. At present I am receiving instruction in the Faith in Belfast and I long for the day when I can share fully in the reception of the Eucharist.

Having grown up in the Church of Ireland and been a member of the 'Fellowship of Vocation' in that communion, I have been trying to work out – to test what God wants me to do. The decision to seek reception back into the Church has been one which has caused both joy and pain. My parents are divided in their feelings. However since I made my break with Anglicanism – I've not been there since the beginning of March – I've felt a welcome peace especially when at Mass.

I'm not sure why I am telling you all this. But it may be because I need to tell you how much Andrew's book has challenged me. Maybe I too, with all my many and continuing sins, am being called to serve Christ as a priest? Maybe not. That thought or is it a call has been recurring like that of the call to Catholicism since I was much younger. Now, nearly 25 – my birthday is 3rd May – with one decision made and being acted on I need to test the other.

Michael Campbell, Belfast

~

I HOPE YOU DON'T MIND me writing to you, but I feel I must. After reading 'Tears at Night Joy at Dawn' (twice in one week!) I just wanted to say an enormous thank you!! I have been deeply moved and touched by such a truly wonderful man as Andrew.

I find myself praying daily for Andrew's soul in heaven, even though I'm sure he doesn't need my prayers. I also ask God to give me some of what Andrew had – that deep, deep faith and trust.

I have so much love for God, and try my best to please him.

I was a lapsed Catholic until four years ago when at the age of thirty-four I found myself very lost. I turned back to

God. The best thing I ever did!

I belong to a lovely parish called St John's where we have a very special, kind priest Fr. Mark.

It was Fr. Mark who lent me this fantastic book, and even though I cried buckets – I've never been so moved.

Once again a great big thank you! For your insight into the joy reading this book would give. God bless you.

Maria Tuff, Luton

~

ENCOURAGED BY YOUR Grace's suggestion given in the Preface to Andrew Robinson's journal, I would like to express my appreciation for letting me know about the marvellous example of this heroic young man. His name is now added to the list of my favourite candidates for canonization (with daily prayer) which includes also the Venerable John Henry Newman and Charlotte Boyd (who restored the Slipper Chapel to Catholic ownership).

The struggle and faith of Andrew have struck a deep chord in me indeed, because I am experiencing similar struggle although much less painful than his. During an operation five years ago my brain was injured and now I have to live with it besides several other problems of health. Just as in the case of Andrew, many people are praying for me and one's faith is put to the test when healing is not coming as Andrew experienced it. In my 78th year I should welcome the idea of death, but because of my post as national chaplain to R.C. Hungarians in G.B., I feel I may pray for healing. But then I have realised as Andrew did that sharing in the suffering of Christ is a sign of God's love, and that is the reason why in my booklet, *Adoration, Reparation, Intercession*, reparation features so prominently, a special need for our time, making atonement for the many sins in our world, in union with our suffering Lord.

Once again, I thank Your Grace for sending me Andrew's journal. I enclose a small donation for Andrew Robinson Young People's Trust.

Fr George Tutto, London

~

I ONLY MET ANDREW once and that was at a UCM National Conference at the National Agricultural College when he and some of his friends came to provide musical entertainment for us. I know I speak for so many of our members when I say that he was unforgettable. There was in him an unmistakable aura of spirituality combined with an infinite joy of life. Our members were all deeply upset when we heard of his subsequent fight against cancer.

I have read the book during the last two days. It has moved me to tears and often to laughter. I have another interest in Andrew's courage and his journey in faith. We too lost our eldest son with cancer some years ago and, although it was a time of deep pain; it was also a time when we received the most enormous love and support and for myself it became a time of a great deepening of my faith. As I too am now involved in a course of chemotherapy for bowel cancer, I have found this book an inspirational testimony to the grace and love of God.

Sheilagh Preston, Sheffield

~

I FOUND ANDREW'S book so uplifting and inspirational, and the depth of his faith unbelievable. I am sure that God's plan for Andrew was what Andrew had wanted to do all along (but maybe not quite in the way Andrew had envisaged) – to tell people of God's total unconditional love for them – a love that even death cannot take away, as he showed in his unshakeable belief in the resurrection. I am convinced that Andrew, by his own suffering, has touched many, many more people than he ever would have done through the priesthood alone. I don't think anybody could read his book without being deeply touched by it. Thank you for inviting him to write it.

Sheila McAleese, Coventry

~

I BOUGHT AND READ today the journal of Andrew Robinson titled 'Tears at Night, Joy at Dawn'. I feel I must accept your invitation to write in response to Andrew's journal.

I am just completing my second year of formation as a candidate for the permanent diaconate. My wife trained as a nurse with specialist skills caring for those with cancer, Oncology. At 37 and keeping my own spiritual journal I felt some sympathy with or allegiance to the life I was reading about. I feel that Andrew's journey is one that once in some way shared by reading his journal has become part of or has added to my spirituality. One cannot remain unaffected by his life and his obvious love of God. He has left a precious gift with us who in a smaller and incomparable way share the path to ministry. I hope and pray that God sees Andrew now as one his Son ordained to his service in the new life he has now – it must be so.

I will be purchasing more copies of Andrew's journal as gifts for friends. His life is like a homily and it should be preached.

Rev. Dr Tony Strike, Fareham

~

AT PRESENT, I AM in full time ministry as a Parish Lay Chaplain in Luton. All my life I have been sure of my vocation to the priesthood.

Since being appointed to my parish here, I have felt so content and sure that I am where God wants me to be. I am so honoured to be able to carry out this ministry.

However, recently, I have felt there is a need to make a decision as to when I will pursue my vocation to the priesthood.

To be honest, as a man of 22, the thought of seminary scares me. Partly because I always hear stories of how awful seminary experience is.

I have always been willing to go to seminary, but just not happy about it.

After reading Andrew's journal, I have found myself experiencing a sense of real calm and willingness to start on this new chapter in my life.

I have been profoundly moved and challenged by this book, and I thank you most sincerely for promoting its publication.

I don't think I have ever read a book from cover to cover in one go. But I simply could not put it down. I would recommend Andrew's journal to anyone, especially anyone thinking of priesthood.

Liam Connolly, Luton

I HAVE JUST READ 'Tears at Night, Joy at Dawn'. I have never read a book like it, it was so inspiring, such faith. I would love to have met this most wonderful young [man]. I know that he went to God. The book had me in tears it was lovely, and it's a book everybody should read, thank you for making it possible to read.

M.A. Doherty, Portsmouth

~

HIS BOOK IS certainly an inspiration. I couldn't put it down and have gone over parts of it again and again.

Mrs. P.C. Ogden, Oxon

~

TAKING YOU UP on your request to write to you after reading Andrew's book, I cannot thank you enough for suggesting he keep the journal.

Truly inspiring, I am sure that God will use it, amongst other things, for the promotions of vocations to the priesthood. Now Vocations Director for Brentwood, I have encouraged the priests of the diocese to read it and to pass it on to others.

Fr Andrew Headon

~

WHILE READING it there were many tears but also much laughter. He was a very refreshingly honest young man who I believe faced death as he faced life with optimistic commitment. He also seems to explain suffering in a very powerful way. His honesty in describing is to be admired and his relationship with God to be envied.

This book needs to be reviewed in our national newspapers so that people can find out in a positive way the meaning and purpose of life and death. It would be interesting to read what some of these cynical critics make of it.

Win Taylor, Worcester

∼

ANDREW'S WONDERFUL descriptions of his trip to Italy, his time in hospital and his general good humour are an inspiration. It also gave him a heightened appreciation of the simple things in life.

Margaret Fowler, West Yorkshire

∼

I WRITE IN REPLY to your preface in the book 'Tears at Night, Joy at Dawn'. I have never read such an extraordinary book on suffering, with Christ on the Cross, and with such faith as Andrew Robinson had. I pray for him now, and please give my love and prayers to Mr & Mrs Robinson and their children. And maybe – please God – the book will bring many more men into the priesthood.

Please accept this little cheque, as a donation to the Andrew Robinson Young People's Trust

Mary Stewart, Preston

~

THERE IS SOMETHING very moving about the death of a young person and Andrew's account is especially so. His faith and cheerfulness are an inspiration and his love for the priesthood. He sounds such a normal young man and, please God, his response will inspire other young men to follow the Lord's call to the priesthood.

Sr Philomena, Wetherby

~

YOUNG ANDREW didn't make it to ordination, yet left us with this awe-inspiring story of faith – a story that has inspired me as a student deacon, and a story which hopefully I am to pass on to others.

Andrew gave us a privileged glimpse into the final months of his life. We feel as though we know him personally, and his friends who stood by him so faithfully, since Andrew's journal is written in such an honest, frank, and often humorous style. We laughed and cried.

Praise too must go to Andrew's mum Stella, for the

courage to finish off the journal on Andrew's behalf. That must have taken some doing!

In answer to his dad Clive's message – I hope that in my ministry as deacon, I can pass on Andrew's message to the sick and dying. I pray that I can share with others Andrew's faith in my ministry.

Rev. Deacon Paul Blinston & Mrs Susan Blinston, Wigan

~

I WISHED TO let you know how very moved I was on reading 'Tears at Night, Joy at Dawn'. A real inspiration of the Holy Spirit to prompt you to ask Andrew to write his journal – its charm, candour, and beauty act as such an inspiration. I was particularly encouraged by his section 'Getting Right With God' – his honesty and humility. I am sure that his testimony will bring a shower of graces down upon your archdiocese and on Oscott. I am myself a few years older than Andrew and now a deacon…... Andrew's commitment and evident path to holiness in his acceptance of his cross shall be a lasting encouragement in my own vocation as monk and (DV) priest.

Br. Alexander, Isle of Wight

~

IT IS WRITTEN so much from the heart that although I never met Andrew I now feel I knew him. Two of our friends were in Andrew's year at Oscott and they have since told me how 'really Andrew' the book is even though it is hard to believe someone could be so close to God and 'contented' or rather 'at peace' in such adversity and suffering. The comments made by others that 'I could not put it down' is certainly true, I have a ten month old son so it was impossible to read it in one go but each time I resumed reading it was like again speaking to a close friend.

I must admit I was filled with tears during the last two chapters (the addendum written so beautifully by Andrew's mother and the words of Andrew's father at the funeral), it was not so much of the sad loss of a life although I did feel an element of losing who would have made such an excellent priest, rather an inspiration that one could trust in God and have such love of life and such little fear of death – he really felt it a blessed honour to suffer as Christ suffered. I was left feeling hopeful that Andrew's life will be an inspiration to others – he is clearly a priest now in heaven.

Mrs. L. Brennan, Surrey

~

I HAVE NOT been a Catholic long, and converted at university. Nevertheless I believe God is calling me to the priesthood. Sometimes this makes [me] happy, but other times scared or frustrated. Like Andrew though I believe I am willing to accept the challenge. I have told very few people about this, besides my spiritual advisor. Yet Andrew's testimony reassures me that in my weakness I shall find strength.

This was not what I planned for my life, and as none of my friends are Catholics I may receive little in terms of encouragement or support. But Andrew's story shows how faith seen through with love is a powerful force.

Douglas Beard, Essex

~

I AM A SEMINARIAN of Holy Spirit Seminary, Queensland. I am in my fifth year and am on pastoral formation year in this parish of All Saints.

I wanted to write to you to say I have just finished reading Andrew Robinson's journal, 'Tears at Night, Joy at Dawn'. In fact, I have just finished reading it a second time and I know I will read it again. I devoured it on the first reading and now I am savoring it on the second.

It was a marvellous book! It is moving, challenging, uplifting and an immense privilege to be allowed to share in Andrew's ponderings, prayers, pain and joy. As a seminarian I found myself wondering how I would be if one of my fellow seminarians were terminally ill. As well, I found myself wondering, what if that were me?

Reading the book also helped me to both wonder at and surrender to God's plan and vision for my life. Like Andrew I believe that God is calling me to the ordained presbyteral ministry yet Andrew did not get there. In fact, God intervened in Andrew's life to change his direction not once but twice. He didn't make it to ordination but through his published journal he will reach and touch countless people, more than all the homilies he might ever have preached, more than all the sacramental events he might have celebrated. I am filled with great heart and faith from Andrew's story that if I surrender to God's will and desire for me, then God will be able to do great things through me and for me.

All Saints Parish, Queensland, Australia

~

I WANT TO THANK YOU for suggesting to Andrew that he should keep a journal of his experiences. I was so moved and inspired by his courage, his faith and the manner in which he accepted his suffering. What an example for all of us. I was moved to tears while reading it.

Sr Eamon SM, Fiji Islands

~

I AM DEEPLY touched by the reading of this account of the life and death of Andrew Robinson. He is certainly measuring up to our namesake, St Andrew, the Apostle. If by chance you are in touch with his family, please express to them my sentiments of love, prayer and support. While it is difficult for a child to precede mother and father in death, they live with the blessed assurance that their Andrew is a companion of the great St. Andrew in heaven. In their sorrow, I wrap them in the mantle of Mary, Our Lady of Sorrows.

Fr Andrew McDonald, Illinois, USA

~

Appendices

Appendix 1

IN JULY 1999 Andrew was at Kidlington Parish on a parish placement. His time there had gone well and he was well liked by the parishioners. After his diagnosis was known, Fr Mervyn Tower informed the parish and a collection was made in aid of Andrew. Andrew was asked what he wanted to do with the money and responded immediately saying he wanted to visit San Giovanni Rotondo – the home in Italy where St Padre Pio lived and died.

Appendix 2

REMARKABLY, FIVE MONTHS to the day of Andrew's death the postcard he sent from San Giovanni to his parents arrived. The postcard brought great comfort and consolation to the Robinson family. It contained the very simple but powerful message: 'Hi Mum and Dad. Missing you. Praying for us all. I love you. Andy XXX! It was like a message from Andrew from heaven!

Appendix 3

MARIA AND HER boyfriend Tom had already planned an around-the-world trip before Andrew became ill and were advised by the specialist that there was no reason for them not to go at that time.

Appendix 4

Beautiful Lady

BEAUTIFUL LADY, we pray, reveal to us the love that you portray. Your words so gentle, O sinless Queen. Your heart so pure, Star of the Sea.

Refrain: Ave Maria, ave…

Our simple words just can't express your radiance and tenderness. Christ's own reflection, to you we sing. Lead us into your Son, our risen King.

Refrain.

O Dear White Rose, O Dear White Rose. Whose petals enfold, enfold in my heart. Please draw me daily, into the centre of your sweetness.

Refrain.

Glossary

Climbing Skiddaw

Famous five

A term of endearment of the group of friends who climbed Skiddaw with Andrew in February 1999.

John

John Bentley, fellow seminarian at Oscott College. Ordained in 2003. Diagnosed with Pics Disease 2006.

Katy

Katy Hogg, Andrew's girlfriend before entering Seminary.

Thanh

Thanh van Nguyen, a fellow seminarian with Andrew at Oscott College who is now a priest in Norway.

Oscotian

A magazine published by Oscott College.

No End in Sight

Q.E.	Queen Elizabeth Hospital, Birmingham.
Chemo	Chemotherapy, a combination of powerful drugs used to kill cancer cells and stop them spreading. Because the drugs are so powerful they have many, very unpleasant and debilitating side effects such as nausea and vomiting, hair loss, depression and weakness.
Anna	Anna Cacy, a friend from the Coventry deanery youth group.
Richard	Andrew's brother.
Sarah	Richard's girlfriend.
Fr Mark	Fr Mark Crisp, Rector of St Mary's College, Oscott, Birmingham. (Given the title 'Monsignor' in 2008).
Maltfriscan	The first Maltfriscans were a group of punk rockers and some other young people living in

and around Maltby, South
Yorkshire. Touched by God's
love and inspired by St Francis
(hence the name, Maltby
Franciscans – Maltfriscans),
they wanted to 'do something'
in thanks for God's love as
revealed in Jesus Christ, the
Saviour. Initially they had
a weekly prayer meeting to praise
and thank God for his love. Later,
a desire to follow and love Christ
in more concrete ways resulted in
the writing of the Maltfriscan
Rule by Maltby's parish priest,
Fr Leonard May. The Community
has grown since then as more
people have felt called to follow
Christ through living out the
Rule. The Community do not
live under one roof but are always
united closely in spirit by their
common calling and obedience to
the Maltfriscan Rule.

A Hidden Despair

San Giovanni
Rotondo　　　　　　　　Shrine in Italy to St Padre Pio.

From Hell to Paradise

Palazzola　　　　　　　Palazzola is about 15 kilometres
outside Rome, close to Ciampino
Airport. Andrew was only due to
finish a course of chemotherapy
the day before they flew out
to Italy, so he would be weak
and not up to too much travel.
Palazzola was a good place to
stop off after the flight from
England. It was also known
to Frs Mark and Mervyn as
the Villa of the English College,
Rome, where students
traditionally spend 3 weeks at
the end of the academic year,
leading to the diaconate
ordinations in July.

PICC Line	Peripherally Inserted Central Catheter – line put into the patient's arm to administer drugs/saline drips/nourishment.
Cardinal Bernardin	Cardinal Joseph Bernardin, Archbishop of Chicago, who died of cancer.
Match of the Day	A much loved and watched Saturday night programme in the UK featuring highlights from the day's football/soccer matches.
Hilda, Arthur, Roger Harry, Gary, Sue, Akka and the Japanese man	Fellow patients at Ward 1, Queen Elizabeth Hospital, Birmingham
Fr Mervyn	Fr Mervyn Tower, Parish Priest of St Thomas More, Kidlington, now at St John's, Banbury. (Given the title 'Canon' in 2010).
Jane, Maggie, Lou, Pete and Collette	Parishioners of St Hugh of Lincoln, Kidlington.

Fr Pat Kilgarriff

Monsignor Kilgarriff, was Rector of the Venerable English College, Rome during Andrew's visit. Now Parish Priest of St Joseph, Malvern.

St Padre Pio

Antonio

Andrew knew Antonio Marcucci from his youth group days in Coventry, but then co-incidentally met up with him at St Hugh's Kidlington, when he went there on a student placement with Fr Mervyn. The further coincidence was that Antonio's friend (Antonio Lucia) ran a family guest house in San Giovanni Rotondo which was made available to them during their stay.

Gerry Bradley

A friend of Andrew's from Coventry youth group days who is now living in Northern Ireland.

Mandy

A friend of Andrew's from

	Coventry youth group days and also from the Maltfriscans.
Richard	A friend of Mandy's who has since died from Leukaemia.
Karl	A friend of Mandy's.
Ann Fellows	A fellow parishioner at St Thomas More, Coventry, who died of cancer in 2001. Andrew read at her funeral on Ash Wednesday.
Steve Rooney	A parishioner of Holy Family, Coventry, who died of Leukaemia.

St Michael's Grotto

Fr Rinaldo	Spiritual Director of Antonio Lucia and Antonio Marcucci.

My Blessed Day

Fr Ermelindo	A friar who lived with Padre Pio.

Is Anyone Listening?

Megan	The daughter of Andrew's mother's friend.

Caroline	Caroline Lyntot who is a nurse Andrew knew through the Maltfriscans.
Kathleen	Kathleen O'Brien is a Maltfriscan and a friend of the Robinson family.
Archbishop Ilsley Secondary School	A Catholic comprehensive school in Birmingham.
Beatrice Upham	A parishioner at St Thomas More, Coventry.
Warren Pearl	A hospice in Solihull.
Paul Edwards	Fellow student at Oscott who is now a priest in the Archdiocese of Birmingham.
Andy Franklin	A classmate at Oscott College, who is now a priest of the Diocese of Wrexham.

Getting Right With God

Greg	Greg McGuire, a long-standing friend of Andrew's.
Leigh-Ann	Greg's partner.

Dan Greg's brother.

**Fay, Andy, Marie-Ann,
Doug, Betty, Sarah,
Patsy, Lilian** Family of Greg and Leigh-Ann

Debbie A friend of Katy.

Mike Green Fellow student at Oscott, now married with a family.

Fr Hugh Fr Hugh Sinclair, Spiritual Director of Oscott College.

Ordination Hopes

Stent pipe An expandable tube, like a large biro spring, made out of mesh, which is inserted into diseased or narrowed body tubes and then widened out in order to try to keep the body tubes open.

James James was an altar server at St Thomas More, Coventry.

Professor David Kerr Professor of Radiotherapy and Oncology at Queen Elizabeth Hospital, Birmingham.

The Call to Priesthood

Maria Andrew's sister. A Youth Officer for the Archdiocese of Birmingham.

SVP-Youth Saint Vincent de Paul Society.

CAYA Catholic Association of Young Adults.

Fr Louis McRaye A former spiritual director at Oscott College, now retired, and working at Our Lady of the Wayside Parish, Shirley.

Andrew's Last Day

Rachel Rachel Thompson, a friend from Coventry deanery youth group.

Mgr Thomas Gavin The Robinson family's late Parish Priest at St Thomas More, Coventry, died 25 Dec 2009.

Fr Jonathan Veasey At the time was resident at St Thomas More, Coventry, and assisted Mgr Tom Gavin in the

	parish. His full-time role in the Diocese is Primary Schools Advisor in the Diocesan RE Department at Coleshill and now also Parish Priest of St John Vianney, Coventry.
Dr Madu Garala	The Robinson family doctor.
Eileen	Eileen Gibney, night nurse at Andrew's bedside, from Sacred Heart parish, Coventry.

Royalties from the sale of *Tears at Night, Joy at Dawn* will be donated to the Andrew Robinson Young People's Trust (Charity Number 1094029).

The Andrew Robinson Young People's Trust is a charitable trust established in Andrew's name to continue and develop his outreach work with disadvantaged young people.

For further details and information on the work of the charity please contact:

Clive Robinson (Chairman)

31 Daventry Road, Coventry CV3 5DJ

Tel: 02476 501579